The Unplanned Lesson

The Unplanned Lesson

HOW TO STOP SEARCHING FOR ACTIVITIES AND START ENGAGING STUDENTS

Ian Roth and Paul Wicking

University of Michigan Press
Ann Arbor

Published in the United States of America by the
University of Michigan Press
Printed and bound by CPI Group (UK) Ltd, Croydon, CR0 4YY

First published December 2023

ISBN 978-0-472-03963-0 (print)
ISBN 978-0-472-22154-7 (e-book)

I dedicate this book to my mother. Though I was never much of an artist, you inspired me to create in my own way.

—Ian

I dedicate this book to Risako, Raiki, and Izumi. You taught me all the important things.

—Paul

CONTENTS

ACKNOWLEDGMENTS

We would like to acknowledge the contributions of Keith McCandless and Henri Lipmanowicz. Your pioneering work on Liberating Structures led to the writing of this book. Your willingness to share what you created made writing it much easier.

We would also like to thank all of the students who participated in the development of this approach. The early stages were doubtless a bit clumsy and we appreciate your patience and honesty.

Finally, thank you to ExpertART for the design of the images that accompany each FERM structure.

Section 1

WHY TO USE STRUCTURE-BASED TEACHING

Chapter 1

A PERFECT PLAN?

Introduction

Perhaps the most pervasive unchallenged rule of the teaching profession is that a lesson must be carefully planned. A solid lesson plan offers predictability, safety, and order, providing a sense of control over the messy business of teaching and learning. At least, that is how it seems. Trainee teachers are taught how to plan a lesson right down to the last minute, often with blow-by-blow directions of what questions to ask and what words to write on the board. Once these trainees get into the real world of teaching, however, they soon discover that sometimes it's just not possible to plan a lesson. This may be due to non-classroom events, such as a sudden change in schedule or being asked to substitute for an absent teacher, or limited time. And even when a lesson is planned, it is not uncommon for that plan to become untenable because it simply doesn't land right. If you've never had a meticulously planned lesson fall flat, you either haven't been teaching for very long or you haven't been paying attention.

Any number of issues can trip up your lesson plan. It could be unforeseen circumstances such as technology trouble or students being unprepared. Perhaps the planned lesson finishes too early, and there is a chunk of class time remaining that needs to be filled. You may be missing half of your students due to a delayed train. Or the class may just be having a low-energy, unwilling-to-engage day. It is times like these when careful preparation not only fails you, it betrays you. The more convinced you are of the necessity of a lesson plan, the more panic inducing it will be to find yourself at the front of a classroom without a viable one. However, experienced teachers know that occasionally these "unplanned lessons" end up being effective and engaging. Flying by the seat of one's pants can produce a dynamism and creative tension all its own. It's often the case that not having a plan makes us more responsive to students' needs, gives us a heightened awareness of being present in the classroom, and forces us to creatively adapt to the immediate situation.

Wouldn't it be great if there was a way to free yourself from the shackles of a lesson plan, unleashing dynamic and creative forces in your classroom while also maintaining some structure and order? That is what this book hopes to help you achieve.

What This Book Is Not

First, this is not a book that advocates being unprepared.

While there are many advantages to leaving a lesson unplanned, one should never be unprepared. Being properly prepared means having an understanding of lesson goals, curriculum objectives, and the needs of the students. Being unplanned means being liberated from rigid expectations for how a lesson should proceed.

Second, this is not a book that promotes the abolition of all lesson plans.

Structured lesson plans can be immensely helpful. They represent how a lesson could flow and guide the selection of content, the choice of activities, and the order in which they are done. The problem that arises with best-laid plans, however, is they often cannot adapt easily to changing classroom dynamics. It is an essential skill of an excellent teacher to be able to abandon the lesson plan when it's not working and to deliberately leave some lessons or parts of lessons unplanned to be more responsive to learner needs and to better achieve learning goals.

Finally, this is not a book of merely fun ideas to use in your classroom.

This point needs to be made and emphasized right at the outset. Certainly, you will find many ideas in this book, and most (if not all) of them will help create a lively learning environment. But the problem with using "fun ideas" in the classroom is that although they may be enjoyable and useful for some limited purposes, they can often just be a distraction from the serious business of teaching and learning. There are few things that will hinder your development as a teacher more than relying on a bag of tricks. What this book provides is a principle-based system that, when practiced earnestly and consistently, will make you a better educator.

The Aim of This Book

This is a book that aims to provide you, the teacher, with ideas to help structure an unplanned lesson so that the inherent chaos of the classroom can be transformed into an asset—the goal is not to eliminate or control chaos but to domesticate it. These ideas will help you to welcome freedom and spontaneity into your language classroom while also remaining focused on curricular objectives. This book proposes a way for you to be responsive and adaptive in the moment while also guiding students toward desired learning outcomes. This is done through a series of ready-to-use structures that are supported by a set of simple, powerful principles.

There are fifty such structures presented in this book, each of which has been designed to engage minds and liberate creativity. We have termed these "FERM" structures, as they are:

> *Flexible.* They can be used with a broad range of lesson content, learner abilities, and class sizes.

Evolvable. They can be made more or less complex as needed to provide an optimal degree of challenge.

Repeatable. They do not lose (and often gain) efficacy with regular use.

Memorable. They are simple, easily remembered, and readily employed.

By attending to these four characteristics, it's possible to transform a series of activities into a coherent but responsive structure. Practicing the approach to teaching presented in this book will allow you to overcome some common challenges faced by both early-career and veteran teachers, such as:

- having insufficient time to make a detailed lesson plan
- teaching from a course book that is ill-suited to learner needs
- realizing in the middle of a lesson that your plan isn't working well
- having very little information about the learners before the course begins
- teaching the same lesson so often it feels stale
- feeling out-of-touch with students' needs
- coasting through lessons on autopilot
- feeling constricted by how to meet the demands of the syllabus

The Organization of This Book

The inspiration for FERM structures is drawn from several diverse fields, with the main ones being second language acquisition (SLA), organizational development, military training, and athletic coaching. Best practices in each of these fields were synthesized and organized according to principles conducive to learning. The first section of this book (chapters 1 to 3) describes the theoretical foundations that gave rise to the FERM approach. It also argues for the educational efficacy of "structures" as opposed to "activities" and goes into some detail regarding the FERM criteria, providing guidelines for teachers interested in creating their own structures.

The second section of the book is a catalogue of fifty structures that can be readily employed in any language classroom. Each structure is accompanied by a simple visual diagram that helps explain the patterns of interaction. Some common classroom or textbook activities that work well with each structure are listed, followed by a written description of its practical implementation. There are also some suggestions for variations to the structures and recommendations for other structures that work well in combination.

The third and final section contains additional material to support you in using the FERM approach. There are some structures that can be used to assess students' understanding and get feedback on their progress, as well as ideas for evolutions to increase complexity or adjust patterns of interaction. We also included some sample lesson sequences which can be used as models for your own lessons.

This volume is a practitioner's handbook, and so it aims to be highly practical. We recommend that you familiarize yourself with the theoretical arguments and ideas in the first section, as this will enhance your ability to apply these structures in your lessons. The second section can be used for quick reference when designing your lessons, either during the planning stage or even while you are teaching. Although we present fifty structures here that have been tested and proven in the classroom, the number of possible structures is limitless. Once you become confident with the approach described in this book, you'll be ready to make your own structures, tailored to suit your personal teaching style and educational context.

Pedagogical Approach

In explaining our pedagogical approach, it may be helpful to use a metaphor. The metaphors you associate with teaching have a significant impact on your classroom.[1] Which metaphors do you employ in understanding the act of teaching a class? Are you a tour guide, constructing a careful itinerary that hits all the most interesting places? Are you a chef meticulously preparing a full course meal, cooking up content that is both delicious and nutritious? Or perhaps you and your students are making the meal together by collaboratively following a recipe. Hopefully, you are not a fire fighter running from one conflagration to the next, left with minor burns for your trouble.

The pedagogical approach described in this handbook can be likened to that of a jazz musician. Before the music begins, some things have already been decided, such as the musical key or the tempo. As the band plays, each musician makes a contribution to the group, listening carefully to what others are doing and responding with what is appropriate in the moment. The final shape of the performance is always somewhat unpredictable, but that unpredictability is entirely expected.

The spontaneity, playfulness, and experimentation of a jazz band can be produced in a classroom to great effect. When the teacher and the learners are listening and responding to each other in the moment, and when everyone feels free to follow intuition or inspiration as the lesson is progressing, the resulting dynamic can

---

1. Lawley and Tompkins say of metaphor that it "describes one experience in terms of another, and in so doing it specifies and constrains ways of thinking about the original experience.... Metaphors are therefore both descriptive and prescriptive. In this way, they can be a tool for creativity or a self-imposed prison." James Lawley and Penny Tompkins, *Metaphors in Mind: Transformation through Symbolic Modelling* (London: The Developing Company Press, 2000), 12.

be a powerful force for learning. When the teacher is too focused on a self-imposed lesson plan, however, new directions and opportunities for learning can be missed.

Of course, some structure is needed, lest it become a shapeless cacophony. The FERM approach entails creating a structure that is firm rather than rigid; in other words, one that is sturdy enough to support lesson objectives and give shape to learning but also flexible and permissive enough to encourage freedom and creativity.

Structure-Based Lesson Design

Structure-based lesson design is not a new concept. Rather, it is one of the oldest educational methods of which we know. In the realm of language education, a common structure-based approach is that of *present, practice, produce* (PPP)—itself a structure that has been recognized and codified for millennia, going back at least to the trivium of ancient Greek liberal arts. This approach to lesson design is familiar fare in many teacher-training programs today, which instruct pre-service teachers to create lesson plans that include strictly sequenced activities intended to move learners through a predetermined route, specifying how much time is to be spent on each activity. While this is helpful for trainee teachers, the danger is that if it is taken to excess, classrooms end up resembling mechanical systems rather than living ones.

Because of this, some educational scholars balk at the idea of structure-based education. For example, Patsy Lightbown and Nina Spada characterize structure-based instructional settings as those in which linguistic items are presented and practiced in isolation, accuracy is given priority over meaningful interaction, and students experience a limited range of discourse types while feeling pressured to speak or write correctly.[2] While we understand and agree with the point they are trying to make, this sounds to us more like "stricture-based education" and is not what we have in mind when advocating for a structure-based approach. The FERM structures described in this book have features contrary to Lightbown and Spada's characterization; that is, linguistic items are practiced in context, meaningful interaction is encouraged, multiple discourse types are encountered, and there is less pressure to produce correct language. Our use of the term "structure" is explained below.

---

2. Patsy Lightbown and Nina Spada, *How Languages Are Learned* (Oxford: Oxford University Press, 2013).

Understanding Structures

"Structure" is a broad concept. As we are using the term, it means a smaller "container" (itself a specialized term in the field of organizational development) that has been intentionally constructed to serve some purpose within a larger context. This container creates a space that is multi-purpose yet biased toward encouraging certain types of interactions. As an illustration, when planning a party, attention must be given to the venue. The size of the room and the number of chairs are crucially important to the kind of party you'll end up having. Too much space will result in physical and psychological distance, while too constricted a space will create discomfort. Having many chairs will encourage people to sit down and so create fixed groups, while having no chairs will encourage standing and mingling. Lighting, music, the position of the buffet table, and the location of the bathrooms are all important factors. A well-designed party space will encourage the guests to relax, mingle, talk, and be fed, all thanks to the careful attention paid to structure. Likewise, a high-quality educational structure will promote behaviors conducive to learning.

As an example, take the FERM structure *Expert Interview*, explained below:

Reporter   **Expert**

One learner acts as an expert on a topic, answering all questions posed by their partner, who acts as an interviewer. The actual degree of expertise possessed by the learner is of no consequence. The "expert" responds to any and all questions with an authoritative answer. Blatantly wrong and/or silly answers are to be encouraged.

Here the structure shapes the interaction: one person asks questions, the other person answers them. In this way, each participant is freed to focus on one element of the dialogue. The topic is taken from the content of that day's lesson, so there is the expectation of some common knowledge. The questioner is likely to push the boundaries of the expert's knowledge and creativity, but both participants are incentivized by the playfulness of the interaction to support one another linguistically (e.g., explaining a word they used so their partner can respond). The communication is meaning focused, the motivation is largely intrinsic, reciprocity plays a role, and, even when the information being communicated is fabricated, the interaction is no less genuine since the rules governing it are common knowledge and the questioner's curiosity collaborates with the expert's creativity to create those fabrications.

High-quality structures also take into consideration the environment (or super-structure) in which they operate. For example, a well-constructed house facilitates both privacy and interaction among its occupants while integrating with larger elements of the environment such as the road system and the natural features of the landscape. A house is a structure, located within a neighborhood, located within a city. Likewise, a task exists within the context of a lesson that is part of a course. No matter how engaging the task, it is poorly constructed or unwisely chosen if it does not interface well with and contribute to the class and course to which it belongs.

Conclusion

A FERM approach to lesson design gives you the tools and the confidence to leave your lessons unplanned. It allows you more flexibility and responsiveness and facilitates learner-centered lessons wherein most (and sometimes all) the content comes from the learners themselves. You'll be able to address students' immediate needs without losing sight of long-term learning goals, and you'll drastically reduce the time you spend planning lessons.

Chapter 2

THE HIDDEN POWER OF STRUCTURES

Structures Rather Than Activities

Ask teachers, "What is the essential ingredient for a successful lesson?," and a very common answer is likely to be, "Good activities." The belief seems to be that finding activities that are appropriate for the group of learners and the content of the lesson will result in student engagement and learning. Among the many things this picture leaves out are the flow and coherence of the lesson—how its parts interact and build on each other rather than just what they individually accomplish. There are many reasons why it's better to think of structures, rather than activities, as the essential building blocks of a successful lesson. Let's explore some ways in which they differ.

Goal Driven vs. Material Driven

Activities are tailored to, and likely inspired by, the material. They are the product of a teacher considering how the material that needs to be covered can be converted into something for the learners to do. Structures, on the other hand, are designed to elicit behaviors and patterns of interaction. Deciding which structure to use is primarily a question of identifying which behaviors will best support the learning of a given set of students at a given time in pursuit of the learning goal.

When thinking in terms of activities, the central question is, "What can I do with this material?" When thinking in terms of structures, however, the guiding question is, "What behaviors practiced in what order will best contribute to achieving the goal(s) of this class?" Instead of allowing hard-to-design-for material to lead the class around, you can determine a material-appropriate goal and bend everything else you are required to cover such that it is heading in the same, goal-appropriate direction.

Long-Lived vs. Short-Lived

When the lesson material changes, most activities—being material-dependent in design—end up being shelved. A key feature of structures, however, is their ability to accommodate a range of material. This means that quality structures can be reused with a variety of lesson content. Furthermore, with each repeated use, the educator can iterate on and refine that structure so that its efficacy increases over time. This is particularly true when combining structures. As you experiment with them, you will find combinations that you rely on more often, you will develop a sense for how they change the dynamics of the class, and you will recognize the opportunities they tend to create. It is better to master a few high-quality, widely applicable tools than to stumble over an ever-expanding collection of limited-use ones.

Familiarity vs. Novelty

Despite the essential role of repetition in learning, as a teacher it is easy to fall into the novelty trap of fetishizing new content and activities. It is hard to say whether this is the result of an honest effort to address student motivation or an attempt by teachers to forestall their own boredom. If you find yourself considering and dismissing possibilities because you already used them, the chances are good that you're thinking in terms of activities rather than structures.

A crucial realization for any educator is that students are not only learning the material, they are learning how to be learners in the context of each class they attend. They are acclimatizing to the classroom culture, adjusting to its assumptions, and formulating their expectations. As a result, there are many benefits to establishing lesson consistency and predictability.

The first of these is that students come to know what to expect and, as a result, experience less anxiety. They are better able to synchronize with and trust one another, if only because they have a shared knowledge of class structure. Having some sense of how one will be expected to act and interact during class, and knowing that this sense extends to one's classmates, reduces the anxiety associated with participation. Common knowledge—the shared knowledge of what knowledge is shared—is the substrate of group identity, without which the members cannot have a sense of belonging. Without belonging, psychological safety suffers, leading to lower levels of engagement and decreased performance.

Not only can familiarity effectively counter the anxiety that, to some degree, accompanies all learning, but it is a necessary precursor of creativity. Too many possibilities can produce paralysis as the individual struggles to keep track of, let alone evaluate, those choices. The best way to promote creativity is with well-designed restrictions that provide direction and discipline to low-stakes, iterated behaviors. To illustrate this, consider which set of instructions would be more likely to result in highly creative output: A) write any kind of poem about anything you like, or B) write three haiku about macaroni and cheese.

Of course, some degree of novelty is good. It prompts the brain to become alert and take notice. Overfamiliarity can demotivate or contribute to a lack of presence. When too many expectations are too consistently met, the experience quickly becomes rote and unengaging. However, a well-designed structure can accommodate a variety of content and combine with an array of other such structures in new and fresh ways. An ideal way to strike the needed balance is to provide learners with familiar structures housing unfamiliar content. Then, as they develop their familiarity with that content, the component structures they are already comfortable with can be combined in unfamiliar ways. By acting on these three axes—component structures, how those structures are combined, and the content that populates them—it is possible to keep learners in the sweet spot between novelty and familiarity.

Repeated Use vs. Single Use

Just as creativity thrives on limitations, it also requires repetition. The most creative athletes and artists are always already masters of the fundamentals. Such mastery is developed through the iterated application of those fundamentals across a span of time and a range of contexts. Allowing learners to repeatedly visit the same effective practice structures gives them a chance to explore the possibilities of those structures. Take the *Hot Seat* structure as an example. In this structure, one student is in the "hot seat" while the other group members fire off questions and follow-up questions (FUQs) as quickly as they can.

The Hot Seat Structure

This structure provides a way to practice grammar points and vocabulary, but it also stresses skills like quick thinking, creativity, and adaptability. Even once the targeted language content (e.g., grammatical structures or vocabulary words) has been mastered, the structure is still able to provide a challenge through the demands it makes on these skills. Each use of the structure results in something unique but also predictable. The students know how the last round went and can try something else the next time.

While adaptive capacity can only be built through experimentation, experimentation is more than just trying something new. It is a cycle that includes feedback and iteration. It is impossible to go through this cycle—to experiment or adapt—if you only have one chance to try something. This is why rather than becoming mindlessly rote, high-quality training modalities gain in value through repeated use.

Time under Tension vs. Time on Task

The concept of *time under tension*—otherwise known as *time under meaningful load*—originates with resistance training but can be applied to the improvement of any skillset. It can be thought of as an evolution of the time-on-task metric that is commonly discussed by teachers. Where time on task refers to the length of time spent actively involved in a task, time under tension "refers to the amount of time a muscle is held under tension or strain during an exercise set."[1]

The problem with time on task is its failure to account for the quality of engagement being exhibited. Students who are trying to decipher the instructions, who are engaged in task-related but not skill-improving activity, or who are performing the task incorrectly are all logging time on task without reaping many benefits. To qualify as time under tension, however, the learners must be working under a sufficiently demanding cognitive load that stresses the appropriate knowledge and skills.

Let's put it in the language of resistance training to explain what we mean. A novice exerciser may spend a great deal of time on task as she checks her routine, decides what movements to do next, struggles with proper technique, and adjusts the resistance to find something appropriate. A veteran exerciser, meanwhile, may complete her workout in a much shorter time, using movements that are executed with good form and appropriate resistance. According to the logic of time on task, the novice has engaged in a better training session. Clearly, this conclusion is absurd.

Time can only be spent well if it's spent on what matters. The manageable size, repetitiveness, and memorability of FERM structures cuts down drastically on teacher talk time as well as on time that qualifies as time on task without being time under tension. There is very little to explain or figure out and there is little chance of error, and each of these further decrease with time and repeated use.

---

1. Emily Cronkleton, "Time under Tension Workouts: Are They More Effective?" accessed March 28, 2021, https://www.healthline.com/health/exercise-fitness/time-under-tension.

Here is what a teacher's instructions might sound like after a few weeks of structure-based lessons:

Teacher: "Okay, let's do a *Hot Seat*. The topic is hobbies. Use this vocabulary".
(Students engage in six to eight minutes entirely time under tension with teacher signaling role changes)

Teacher: "Now, take five minutes to make three *50/50 Questions* about hobbies. Use the same vocabulary."
(Students engage in five minutes largely time under tension)

Teacher: "Next, please get a new partner, and ask those questions. Guess whether the answers you receive are *Fact or Fiction.*"
(Students engage in six to eight minutes largely time under tension)

In this example, the teacher has spoken for around twenty seconds while the learners have logged approximately twenty minutes of time under tension. This ratio is unlikely to be maintained over the course of an entire lesson, but is not unrealistic for significant portions of any given class.

Summary

Here, then, are the ways in which structures are distinct from activities.

Structures	Activities
Designed to elicit behaviors and outcomes	Designed to suit the material
Accommodate a broad range of content	Accommodate a limited range of content
Improve with repeated use	Likely grow stale with repeated use
Promote familiarity	Promote uncertainty
Work best in combination	Stand alone
Encourage experimentation	Encourage conservatism
Concerned with time under tension	Concerned with time on task

The Criteria

As explained briefly in the introduction, the FERM structures presented in this book qualified for inclusion by satisfying four criteria. Each structure is *flexible, evolvable, repeatable,* and *memorable.* The importance of each has, to some extent, already been explored. This section will define these qualities in more detail for the benefit of those who seek to design their own FERM structures.

Flexible

A well-designed structure is flexible in three distinct ways: content, ability level, and scale. First, the structure is flexible in terms of content. With little to no modification, it should be possible to plug in a broad range of content and proceed. Obviously, it is not possible for a structure to be perfectly appropriate for every kind of content, so a bit of judgment is required. However, if a would-be structure needs to be described by the kind of content that is used with it (e.g., this is for giving directions or talking about hobbies), it likely does not satisfy this aspect of the flexibility criteria.

Second, the structure is flexible in terms of ability levels. Clearly, you do not want to create new, ability level–appropriate structures for each class, but the diversity of ability that exists within a single class should be considered as well. While a group of learners may operate at a predictable level when working with certain content, a different content chunk may reveal an unpredictably different ability landscape. Both individual learners and groups of learners can display wide variation in knowledge, experience, and skill. The competencies of individuals will vary according to context, as will the competency of the group. Having a familiar set of structures will help to flatten what may be an uneven ability landscape, but familiarity can only be achieved if those structures are flexible enough to accommodate such differing ability levels.

A well-designed structure should also be flexible in terms of scale, since creating new, group size–appropriate structures for each class would be highly inefficient. Furthermore, even in a single class, there will be fluctuations in attendance. Fortunately, many small group communicative structures are inherently flexible in this way. Pair work can just as easily be done in a class of eight as a class of forty. The most likely snag shows up when the structure requires the use of shared resources. If the structure requires a whiteboard for each group and only two are available for use, the structure is not very size flexible. It is also useful to note that mixing group sizes is an easy way to vary the feel of a structure. The same structure employed in groups of four as opposed to pairs will change the emphasis and the nature of the resulting engagement. So, flexibility along this dimension will contribute to a structure's usability.

Finally, though not exactly a requirement for satisfying this criteria, it can only benefit educators to keep in mind the role that digitally mediated learning has come to play in many educational contexts. A teacher who collects structures that only work in person is making themselves vulnerable to disruption. Many of the structures included in this book will work over a video conference call exactly as written.

Some will not. But there are just as many structures that will benefit or even depend on this kind of learning environment. We need only keep our eyes open for them.

Evolvable

Well-designed structures accommodate modification. This is an important, though not always necessary, characteristic if they are to achieve the learner level flexibility described above. Perhaps more so, evolvability allows for the gradual increases in complexity required to provide appropriate challenges to learners whose abilities continue to develop. Progressing from simple interactions to ever more complex ones is a reliable way to facilitate learning. As educator and author Parker Palmer points out, the essence of learning lies in the increasing complexity of the relationship between learner and learned.[2]

An evolvable structure is one that can be either modified through evolutions or used in combination with other structures. An example evolution would be to advance from students stating their opinions to stating and supporting those opinions. An example combination would be having the learners start with a *Quote Search* (finding a topic-relevant quote that they agree or disagree with) and then use it to write something for an *R-R-R* (presenting to three people by *reading* what they wrote, then by *referring* to what they wrote, and finally by *remembering* what they wrote).

Evolvability is a crucial characteristic as it allows the educator to craft a wide array of learning experiences despite relying on a limited bank of structures. It becomes possible to do more with less, which means increased efficiency and decreased focus on the tools themselves. As well-designed structures are able to be combined in various ways, this enables learners to engage in demanding, multi-stage interactions with the material, transitioning smoothly from one task to the next.

Repeatable

One of the core principles undergirding a FERM structured approach to lesson design is that high-quality training methods increase in value as they are repeatedly used. As previously stated, this increasing value can be partially attributed to the level of task comfort learners develop, which allows them to focus on exploring and employing the content. They do not need to split their resources between learning the content and learning the task—the latter has become functionally invisible. Any errors will be useful errors—that is, they will be content use errors rather

---

2. Parker Palmer, *To Know as We Are Known: Education as a Spiritual Journey* (San Francisco: Harper, 1983).

than misunderstandings. Additionally, both the comfort of a well-known task and repetitive engagement in that task support creative experimentation. Single-use activities require learners to develop a shallow understanding of how to function in a narrow, often contrived context. Well-designed structures, repeatedly used, allow them to develop a deep understanding of highly functional skills.

This last point is crucial: the repeatability of the structure is associated with its ability to facilitate the development of higher order thinking and communicative skills (sometimes referred to as "transversal competencies" or "twenty-first-century skills"). There are, for example, a number of FERM structures that involve story-telling. This is not only a skill that can be ever further refined, it is also practical. Compare this with activities like reading a scripted conversation or completing a vocabulary cloze exercise. Activities such as these fail to develop similarly useful, perpetually refinable skills, which is why, despite initially enjoying them, learners are likely to greet subsequent use with a dubious, "We're doing this again?" In contrast, even if you use the same FERM structures dozens of times with the same group of learners during the course of a year, each time can be unique and engaging.

Memorable

While this is the most straightforward of the criteria, it is nevertheless crucially important. Structures that satisfy this criterion can typically be communicated in under a minute and have catchy monikers to help students remember them. The simple directions and monikers associated with each structure allow for ready deployment. This has several benefits, the most obvious being that it limits the amount of teacher talk time.

Reducing teacher talk time is important because there are very few skills that can be effectively learned by listening. Lectures, then, are more effective for broadcast-ing information than for facilitating learning. For the complexity of the relationship between learner and learned to grow, the learner needs to transform the content to be learned from a collection of information points into a network of relationships. This means manipulating it in a variety of ways across a range of contexts. It also means con-necting the content to prior experiences and future intentions. This can be achieved efficiently if the learner is readily able to move through a series of interactions, shifting smoothly and with considered timing from one to the next. Long explanations take the focus off the goal and cut down on time under tension. The memorability of FERM structures allows the teacher to build up and maintain lesson momentum, not only by quickly switching at the natural conclusion of a structure but by making it easy to switch away from a structure that is taking too long or not working well.

Additionally, memorability facilitates spaced repetition and interleaving as it allows the teacher to switch from one kind of practice to another before going back to the first one. For instance, if you want to focus on a set of vocabulary words, try choosing a single FERM structure for the purpose of training that set, then insert that structure throughout the lesson, layering it between the other content covered, regardless of whether it is related to the vocabulary. This is called interleaving and might result in a lesson sequence like this:

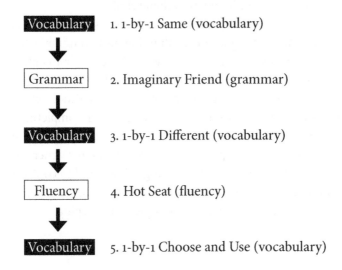

Vocabulary — 1. 1-by-1 Same (vocabulary)

Grammar — 2. Imaginary Friend (grammar)

Vocabulary — 3. 1-by-1 Different (vocabulary)

Fluency — 4. Hot Seat (fluency)

Vocabulary — 5. 1-by-1 Choose and Use (vocabulary)

This pattern and flow only work when the structures in use can be readily deployed. Such interleaving and spaced repetition are extremely effective for strengthening recall, but this effectiveness relies on the learners being able to switch quickly, even abruptly, back to the previous knowledge set. The more time they have to prepare for the switch, the less urgently the information will be called to mind. This will weaken the message being sent to the brain that the information is important and should be retained.

Something else that can help the memorability of structures is visual aids. Along with the written explanations of the structures, we have included visual depictions of how the structures look in action. Should you make your own structures in the future, keep in mind the power of engaging multiple senses to increase memorability.

A note about memorability in the context of digitally mediated learning environments: structures that satisfy this criteria lend themselves especially well to the use of breakout rooms. Because the teacher cannot easily call the entire class to attention in order to provide next-step instructions without dissolving and then recreating those rooms, having a set of structures that are common knowledge contributes greatly to the smooth functioning of a lesson. The teacher should be able to give a series of structure-based instructions (e.g., "Start by doing a *One-by-One* with these words, then go into *Choose and Use*, and finish with two minutes each of *Take your Pick*. I'll signal the changes by messaging everyone."). Or, it may be possible to give next structure instructions through something like a "broadcast to all" function (e.g., "Alright everyone, now switch to *Hot Seat*").

Checklist for designing a FERM structure

Use this checklist to help you when designing your own FERM structures.

Is it flexible?

- ☐ Can it be used with a broad range of different content?
- ☐ Can it be used with learners of low-level and high-level ability?
- ☐ Can it be used with classes of different sizes?

Is it evolvable?

- ☐ Can it be made more, or less, complex?
- ☐ Can the level of difficulty be increased as learners become more proficient?
- ☐ Can it be combined easily with other structures?

Is it repeatable?

- ☐ Can skill in using the structure be improved through repeated use?
- ☐ Can learners do it many times and produce different outcomes?
- ☐ Can it encourage creative experimentation?

Is it memorable?

- ☐ Can it be communicated in under a minute?
- ☐ Can the rules of interaction be easily understood?
- ☐ Can it be summed up with a catchy moniker?

Chapter 3

CREATION THROUGH COMBINATION

Theoretical Foundations

The theoretical foundation for the approach taken in this book comes from a combination of principles found within the field of second language acquisition (SLA) and elsewhere. Within the field of SLA, we draw heavily on the principles of communicative language teaching. From outside this field, we have been influenced by the theories and practices associated with organizational development, military training, and athletic coaching. Although the benefit of drawing lessons from such disparate fields may not be immediately apparent, consider first the power of multidisciplinary thinking, and second the enormous resources that have been invested in business, defense and sport.

First, practical innovation almost always comes from multidisciplinary thinking. This is because expertise in a single field comes at a cost. Expertise does provide greater clarity and detail in a narrow field of vision, but this comes at the expense of seeing the periphery and the possibilities that lie just outside one's focus. What a multidisciplinary perspective lacks in detail, it makes up for in the breadth of potential to connect, combine, and apply knowledge from outside one's field. It takes as its subject the adjacent possible—the realm in which all currently available improvements and innovations reside.[1]

Second, the amount of time and money invested by large corporations, militaries, and professional sports teams to better understand skill acquisition and performance dwarfs that of SLA-focused researchers and academic organizations. It is not even close. Add to this the fact that the former are staking so much more on the effectiveness of their methods. Whereas less-than-optimal classroom practices may cost test points, flawed military practice costs lives, faulty corporate strategy costs jobs, and weak sports performance costs money and glory. The more dire the consequences of failure, the greater the commitment to producing results. Language teachers can benefit enormously from considering the principles and practices of these fields in addition to those of SLA.

---

1. See, for example, Stuart Kauffman, *At Home in the Universe: The Search for Laws of Self-Organization and Complexity* (Oxford: Oxford University Press, 1995); Steven Johnson, *Where Good Ideas Come From: The Natural History of Innovation* (New York: Riverhead Books, 2010).

Second Language Acquisition

There are a number of theoretical principles from SLA that contribute to the foundation for our pedagogical approach. The first principle concerns the nature of second language knowledge. In order to achieve competency in a language, two kinds of knowledge are needed: explicit and implicit.[2] Explicit knowledge concerns what a person knows *about* language, such as rules of grammar and meanings of words. This knowledge is conscious, so that learners are aware that they possess it. Implicit knowledge, by contrast, is largely unconscious. It focuses on making meaning in communication rather than the forms of language. In other words, language ability is determined by knowledge of essential items such as grammar and vocabulary, as well as skill in actually using that knowledge to communicate. In order to acquire both kinds of knowledge, a combination of explicit and implicit instruction is needed when studying a second language.[3] Effective language learning lessons are structured to provide explicit and implicit instruction such that they reinforce and support each other.

One way to do this is through skill practice and skill application. Skill practice results from actions that are narrowly focused, appropriate, challenging, and iterated—technically referred to as deliberate practice, or as controlled practice in the teaching literature.[4] This kind of practice is unlikely to arise organically in real world settings but can be orchestrated in the classroom to build explicit knowledge. Skill application, also known as free practice, requires the learner to manage a broader range of possibilities and, consequently, benefits from contextual elements and reflection. Communicative tasks have been successful in developing language competence through skill application in meaning-focused communication. Learners benefit from classrooms in which there are opportunities to build explicit and implicit knowledge through the practice and application of language skills.

The second principle from SLA is that feedback is a crucial element in language learning, as it is with all learning.[5] The classroom is ideal for skill development as it is rich in feedback. The musician knows when they play a wrong note, as they get instantaneous feedback from the sound of their instrument. By contrast, language

---

2. Rod Ellis, Shawn Loewen, Catherine Elder, Hayo Reinders, Rosemary Erlam, and Jenefer Philp, *Implicit and Explicit Knowledge in Second Language Learning, Testing and Teaching* (Bristol: Multilingual Matters, 2009).

3. Shawn Loewen, *Introduction to Instructed Second Language Acquisition,* 2nd ed. (New York: Routledge, 2020).

4. Nasrin Altuwairesh, "Deliberate Practice in Second Language Learning: A Concept Whose Time Has Come," *International Journal of Language and Linguistics* 4, no. 3 (2017): 111–115.

5. John Hattie and Helen Timperley, "The Power of Feedback," *Review of Educational Research* 77, no. 1 (2007): 81–112; Shaofeng Li, "The Effectiveness of Corrective Feedback in SLA: A Meta-Analysis," *Language Learning* 60, no. 2 (2010): 309–365.

learners cannot as readily identify when they have used a wrong word or produced messy grammar. For this reason, externally sourced feedback is crucial for noticing errors and improving performance when learning language. This can come from a variety of sources, such as the confused look on the face of the person they are speaking with or an explicit correction from the teacher. Although the best situations for skill application occur in real world settings, these are not always reliable or readily available. Real life situations can, however, be effectively recreated in classroom settings. Rather than waiting for a conversation that satisfies the desired criteria to come about organically, that exact conversation can be created as often as needed. The reusing and recycling of grammar and vocabulary, which is crucial for language acquisition, can be stage-managed in the classroom.[6] FERM structures create interactions where learners can practice and apply their knowledge and skills, get immediate feedback on performance, and then have an opportunity to use that feedback to improve.

Third, authentic interactions are preferrable to manufactured ones. Although the interactions in a classroom are stage-managed (as mentioned above), they can still require authentic communication, and linguistic abilities are developed through genuinely communicative activity. This has been the premise of the widespread communicative language teaching approach, which prioritizes meaning-focused communication over form-focused production.[7] When classroom interactions are structured so that there is a negotiation of meaning, students learn to overcome breakdowns in communication through various strategies—such as comprehension checks, contextual cues, elaboration, and requests for clarification—all of which aid second language acquisition.[8] FERM structures aim to organize classroom interactions so that such negotiations of meaning take place.

Authentic communication spurs higher order thinking processes and is inherently engaging, thereby supporting increased motivation. When such communication is cooperative or involves learners collaborating together, motivation is boosted even further.[9] Authentic interaction also encourages critical and creative thinking, which reveals and leverages the knowledge that the class (including the teacher) is collectively unaware it possesses.

---

6. Paul Nation, *Learning Vocabulary in Another Language* (2nd ed.) (Cambridge: Cambridge University Press, 2013).

7. Rod Ellis, *Reflections on Task-Based Language Teaching* (Bristol: Multilingual Matters, 2018).

8. Michael Long, "The Role of the Linguistic Environment in Second Language Acquisition," in *Handbook of Second Language Acquisition*, ed. William Ritchie and Tej Bhatia (San Francisco: Academic Press, 1996), 413–468.

9. Zoltán Dörnyei, *Motivational Strategies in the Language Classroom* (Cambridge: Cambridge University Press, 2011).

Fourth, classrooms are complex systems and so are well served by a complexity lens. As Diane Larsen-Freeman and Lynne Cameron have argued, this entails acknowledging that: (a) everything is connected; (b) language is dynamic; (c) co-adaptation is a key dynamic; and (d) teaching is essentially managing these dynamics of learning.[10] Larsen-Freeman and Cameron acknowledge that a complexity approach to language teaching does not immediately translate into a complexity method. Prescribed techniques only limit the activity of teachers and learners and so are not in keeping with the guidelines provided by complexity theory. The use of FERM structures is an approach (not a method) that is flexible enough, and works to heighten teacher responsiveness to such a high degree, that it adequately manages the complex dynamics of learning. Teachers whose lessons are informed by complexity theory will seek to use a range of activities and techniques to facilitate learning, but these activities and techniques will benefit from some kind of structure to hold them together and channel them toward learning goals. A FERM approach can provide that structure.

The skillful management of complex systems demands a heuristic approach rather than an algorithmic one—that is, principles and rules of thumb, with their adaptability and responsiveness, are more functional than rigid formulas and linear, step-by-step processes intended to produce predetermined outcomes. When lesson content is related to formative assessment, educational researcher Wynne Harlen asserted, "What a teacher needs is not a prescribed lesson content but a set of strategies to deploy according to what is found to be appropriate on a particular occasion."[11] The FERM structures in this book provide highly adaptable strategies that respect the complex ecology of the classroom environment, supporting the teacher's efforts to manage the dynamics of learning.

By giving precedence to teacher freedom and responsiveness, our approach is perhaps somewhat similar to that of Dogme in ELT as advocated by Luke Meddings and Scott Thornbury in their book *Teaching Unplugged*.[12] This approach was born from a desire of some language teachers to "free themselves from a dependency on materials, aids and technology, and to work with nothing more than the 'raw materials' provided by the people in the room."[13] The three core precepts of the Dogme approach are that teaching is (1) *conversation-driven*, (2) *materials-light*, and (3) *focused on emergent language*. Many of the structures in this book align with these

---

10. Diane Larsen-Freeman and Lynne Cameron, *Complex Systems and Applied Linguistics* (Oxford: Oxford University Press, 2008).

11. Wynne Harlen, "On the Relationship between Assessment for Formative and Summative Purposes," in John Gardner, ed., *Assessment and Learning* (2nd ed.) (London: Sage, 2012), 91.

12. Luke Meddings and Scott Thornbury, *Teaching Unplugged* (Surrey, UK: Delta Publishing, 2015).

13. Meddings and Thornbury, *Teaching Unplugged*, 7.

precepts, making them compatible with the Dogme philosophy. The main point of difference is that, with our approach, some allowance is given for the use of teaching materials, such as coursebooks. While it is completely feasible to run a FERM lesson without any materials, aids, or technology, there are also ways to incorporate these into the lesson when the teacher deems it expedient or the syllabus requires it.

Organizational Development

The second major inspiration for FERM lesson design comes from the field of organizational development in general, and *Liberating Structures* (LS) in particular. These structures are described by their creators, Henri Lipmanowicz and Keith McCandless, as "an alternative way to approach and design how people work together."[14] Essentially, LS is a toolbox of frameworks that can be used and combined to guide how groups of people interact and engage with each other. As the name implies, the magic of LS is that they serve to encourage individuals within groups to interact more synergistically and, by so doing, supercharge creativity. By designing interactions with carefully considered constraints, LS-based interactions result in emergent, unpredictable outcomes.

There are currently thirty-three microstructures that comprise the LS canon. Most commonly, they find use in organizational settings as they have been shown to contribute positively to organizational culture and performance, in part by leveraging the knowledge of participants to uncover better strategic options. According to the authors, the development of a group's internal confidence—the sense that the group is capable of identifying and implementing its own solutions to the problems it faces—often goes underdeveloped for two reasons.

> One, many leaders…don't realize how smart their organization as a whole is and can be and, two, they and those below them haven't learned how to liberate and tap into their organization's collective intelligence and creativity…. An organization's collective capacity comes in three layers: what the organization knows it knows, what it doesn't know it knows, and what it has the potential to invent. Only the first layer is visible to leaders.[15]

Many, if not all, of the authors' observations apply directly to foreign language classrooms. In this context, learning is not an individual endeavor. The best resources available are the other learners. The teacher may do many things to evaluate what the class knows, but he or she will never be able to completely grasp the entire

---

14. Henri Lipmanowicz and Keith McCandless, "Liberating Structures," accessed March 6, 2023, liberatingstructures.com

15. Henri Lipmanowicz and Keith McCandless, *The Surprising Power of Liberating Structures* (Liberating Structures Press, 2014), 33.

knowledge and potential of any group of learners. Though "organization" is not the best word to describe a class, "team" is both entirely appropriate and readily substituted into the picture painted by Lipmanowicz and McCandless. A class is a learning team and getting the most out of any team is not a question of motivation but of engagement, which is itself a function of internal confidence. This is precisely the outcome LS are designed to produce.

Here are two examples: the first is of LS in an organizational setting and the second example shows how the LS principles can be applied in foreign language classrooms. First, imagine a team that is struggling to meet its deadlines. The manager in charge of the team might once have been tasked with the expert role of diagnosing the problem and prescribing a solution—say, "the team lacks motivation, so let's tweak the incentives a bit to get them going." The LS practitioner, in contrast, treats *the team members* as the experts. They may employ a structure like *15% Solutions*, in which each participant seeks to answer the questions, "What is my 15 percent? Where do I have discretion and freedom to act? What can I do without more resources or authority?," before sharing and exploring those responses in small groups. The result may be that the group collectively identifies the multiple channels of communication being used (e.g., email, bulletin board, team chat) as contributing to missed messages and, thereby, impaired team performance. They decide to restrict and clarify these channels in a sensible way. This is not a solution any single one of them could have predicted, least of all the manager. It emerged from the friction and synthesis of the individuals' experiences and ideas, all of which were made possible by the thoughtful design and implementation of LS structures that gave the teammates room to explore but limited them so they would explore together.

Now let's look at a classroom example. Say, for instance, the syllabus dictates that you cover language associated with job interviews. You might use the FERM structure *Hot Seat* (multiple learners interview one learner for a set period of time) to practice the language through role play. This leads into *Diamond 9* (learners formulate nine answers and order rank them), guided by the question, "What aspect of a job is most important to the members of this class?" Several groups rank a hybrid online/in-person work environment as their guess for most important. The textbook, which was written several years ago, does not include any language related to remote or hybrid working styles. So, you have the learners do *Unique Questions* (compose some questions about a given topic that no other group will think of) to create a pool of questions that employ the language from the book to ask about aspects of remote and hybrid work. These questions are then integrated, along with the existing material, into the remainder of the lesson. This is the kind of emergent content that keeps learners engaged, but it only becomes accessible when teachers give up thinking they know what the learners need, and when the textbook—the ultimate out-of-touch manager—is treated as a reference rather than a roadmap.

Many of the LS are appropriate for classroom use, and some of them (where noted) have been adapted and included as FERM structures in this book. According to a study testing the educational applications of LS, they are "easy to implement, increase participation, have the potential to enhance learning and can represent an effective pedagogical alternative to traditional lecture-centered classrooms.... LS hold the creative potency to enhance both the instructor pedagogical experience and the student learning experience."[16]

While the principles are applicable to any classroom, a large portion of the LS microstructures do not readily lend themselves to use with language learners. This was one motivation for developing the FERM approach—to smuggle the insights of LS into a language learning context in hopes of increasing learner engagement and uncovering more of the latent capabilities of our classes.

Military Training

The third source of inspiration is the training programs used regularly in military settings to develop high-level practical skills in short periods of time. For some readers, this may be an attractive proposition. For others, it may cause concern. To those in the latter group, please consider whether your opinion of the source is a valid reason for dismissing the lesson. Militaries have more funding and need for rapid skill training than any organizational sector on the planet. The chances are good that they know what works.

Military training is designed according to three principles that apply equally well to the language classroom: (1) focus on the fundamentals, (2) maintain realism, and (3) repeat until standards are met.[17] Trainers stick with a chosen training modality until a requisite level of competence can be reliably demonstrated. This triggers an evolution in the training. Evolutions are characterized by the adding or removing of elements such that the learner faces additional challenge. Here's an example: learning to jump from a plane is a multistage process that begins with Ground School, where the trainee learns how to land as safely as possible. This consists of first practicing the skill with no added elements, then jumps are performed from low platforms, the height of which is gradually increased. Next, the landing surface goes from sand to gravel to earth. Finally, the jumps are made from zip lines to add directionality to the fall. Only after graduating from these evolutions are parachutes introduced.

––––––––––––––––––––

16. Arvind Singhal, Lauren Perez, Kristin Stevik, Erik Monness, and Peer Jacob Svenkerud, "Liberating Structures as Pedagogical Innovation for Inclusive Learning: A Pilot Study in a Norwegian University," *Journal of Creative Communications* 15, no. 1 (2020): 1.

17. Don Rose, "Unit Training Management." *NCO Journal* (March, 2020): 1–5, accessed March 30, 2023, https://www.armyupress.army.mil/Portals/7/nco-journal/images/2020/March/Unit-Training/unit-training-management.pdf.

Such evolution-based learning is effective for two main reasons. First, it keeps the focus on the content rather than on the training methodology. Participants rarely need to pause their skill-focused work so they can learn the next training routine. New routines are most often evolved versions of familiar ones (hence the name *evolutions*). Second, this approach strives to keep the learner working at the edge of their ability by ensuring that the level of challenge is adjustable and, therefore, responsive to the participant's current level. This is an application of Vygotsky's arguments about the Zone of Proximal Development, which postulate that the most rapid and reliable skill development happens when the learner is working at a level of difficulty that slightly exceeds what they are able to do without assistance.[18] Stephen Krashen's concept of comprehensible input is similar, though less applicable since its focus is on input.[19]

Engaging the learner in deliberate practice is the primary focus. According to Anders Ericsson, this is practice that is repetitive, challenging, and that targets micro-behavioral components of a larger skill.[20] Effective training is not characterized by novelty but by ensuring that the drills being employed specifically address the behaviors that need to be improved at an appropriate level of challenge. Complex skills, such as communicating in a foreign language, can only be reliably built through the development of micro-skill competencies that are combined in increasingly complex and varied ways. This is not to suggest that the development of language competency is in any way a rigid or predetermined process. Rather, it is an organic process of trial and error through which smaller spaces of competency are developed and networked together to create a more comprehensive map that itself is in constant flux as the language evolves, the context changes, and the learner makes revisions.

These training modalities emphasize realism. For military training, this means squad tactics are often practiced in the midst of loud noises and rubber bullet fire from an opposing team. Perfect execution in a safe, controlled environment does not require the same cognitive operations and, thus, would set the trainees up for failure when faced with the chaos of a battlefield. In the second-language classroom, clinically controlled practice similarly offers limited transferability to a conversational context. Therefore, there is not a single FERM structure in this book that relies entirely on memorization or on prefabricated practice dialogues. Each FERM structure is characterized by aliveness—the unexpected, real-time demands and feedback common to most kinds of communication. Each one makes communicative demands on the learners, ensuring that communicative improvements will follow.

---

18. Lev Vygotsky, *Mind in Society: The Development of Higher Psychological Processes* (Cambridge: Harvard University Press, 1978).

19. Stephen Krashen. *Explorations in Language Acquisition and Use* (Portsmouth: Heinemann, 2003).

20. Anders Ericsson, Ralf Krampe, and Clemens Tesch-Römer, "The Role of Deliberate Practice in the Acquisition of Expert Performance," *Psychological Review* 100, no. 3 (1993): 363–406.

Athletic Coaching

The principles of coaching are the final source of inspiration for our approach. First among these is the need to coach both the individual players and the team. If your team's performance is the sum of the best efforts your players can put forth, you are not a very good coach. A team is a system, as is a class—and one defining characteristic of systems is that they are more than the sum of their parts. Maximizing this synergistic effect depends on improving the quality of the relationships between the parts, be they players or students. The first hurdle to successfully addressing this is creating psychological safety, which is the belief that contributing ideas, asking questions, raising concerns, and making mistakes will not result in punishment or humiliation.[21] Creating psychological safety means attending to four areas: tribe, expectation, rank, and autonomy (TERA).[22] The structures presented in this book address each of these areas.

Tribe is the sense of belonging. As a condition, it must be satisfied before individual performance can be expected, because the unconscious mind first needs convincing that this particular social space is a safe one in which to make an effort.[23] Particularly in the language classroom, the creation of a cohesive group is a crucial element for supporting learning.[24] By providing a shared but peculiar vocabulary for the group to regularly use (see "Memorability" in Chapter Two), FERM structures support this sense of belonging. In addition, these structures facilitate shared experiences, authentic get-to-know-you interactions, low-level managed conflicts, and coordinated action. Each of these contributes in its own way to the development of a tribal identity.

Expectation is serviced by FERM structures as learners are not constantly dealing with new demands in the form of single-use activities. They generally know what they will be doing. Likewise, they have a strong sense of how their contributions will be received. These work together to encourage a belief that they will be successful in completing the task; and increasing learners' expectations of success is one key to generating initial motivation in language learning.[25]

Part of the *rank* component is taken care of by the formal nature of classroom environments. The educator occupies a higher rung than the learners. Of course, an educator who fails to address the other elements of TERA will soon find their functional authority falling short of their formal authority. It also behooves the

---

21. Amy Edmonson, "Psychological Safety and Learning Behavior in Work Teams," *Administrative Science Quarterly* 44, no. 2 (1999): 350–83, accessed March 13, 2023, https://doi.org/10.2307/2666999.

22. Michael Bungay Stanier. *The Coaching Habit* (Toronto: Box of Crayons Press, 2016).

23. Daniel Coyle. *The Culture Code* (New York: Bantam Books, 2019).

24. Zoltán Dörnyei and Tim Murphey, *Group Dynamics in the Language Classroom* (Cambridge: Cambridge University Press, 2003).

25. Dörnyei, *Motivational Strategies in the Language Classroom*.

educator to be realistic about the organic nature of hierarchies. Despite the learners nominally occupying the same rung on the hierarchy, the power and influence of each class member is continually shifting and evolving. The best way to address these developments is to ensure that everyone's contributions shape how things develop—that everyone has a seat at the table. FERM structures are designed with this in mind, giving each learner a clear role and valuing everyone's contributions.

Autonomy is the feeling of having some control over what you do and how you do it. A FERM approach accommodates this in two ways. First, most of the structures are divergent as opposed to convergent in character. That is, they afford the possibility of many correct solutions. In this way, learners are invited to choose their contribution. They are asked to be creative, to draw from their own experiences, and to ask questions they want answered. Second, the inherent flexibility of each structure promotes autonomy. Rather than being mere observers, learners become aware that their level of participation affects how the lesson takes shape.

By attending to the TERA concerns, a good coach curates psychological safety for their team which, in turn, is a precursor for adaptive, innovative performance.[26] Of course, this sort of performance also depends on the pedagogical style employed by the teacher. Again, the field of coaching provides some valuable lessons.

Effective coaching is less teaching than it is facilitating. Rather than dispensing lessons, effective coaches strive to support learning. This means honoring each learner as a locus of meaning making. It means listening rather than lecturing. It means asking instead of answering. It means highlighting successes rather than failures. You cannot ensure that each of your students will learn what you want to teach them. Rather, you should expect that none of them will. Accepting this frees you to support the learning trajectories they are already on.

Good coaching is also characterized by the skilled provision of feedback followed by an opportunity for the learner to integrate that feedback. The education field has also long extolled the role of feedback as essential to improving learning.[27] The best feedback specifically, but non-judgmentally, identifies what the learner is doing right and what they can do to improve. The balance between reinforcing and correcting feedback should lean heavily toward the former to avoid demotivating the learner. And feedback without an opportunity to apply it is wasted breath. One correct execution does not override multiple incorrect ones. A good coach gives learners more practice doing things right than they had repetitions doing it wrong.[28] This is where

---

26. Amy Edmonson, *The Fearless Organization: Creating Psychological Safety in the Workplace for Learning, Innovation, and Growth* (Hoboken: John Wiley & Sons, Inc., 2018).

27. Marai Araceli Ruiz-Primo and Susan Brookhart, *Using Feedback to Improve Learning* (New York: Routledge, 2018).

28. Doug Lemov, Erica Woolway, Katie Yezzi, and Dan Heath. *Practice Perfect: 42 Rules for Getting Better at Getting Better* (San Francisco: Jossey-Bass, 2012).

the deploy-ability and bite-sizedness of FERM structures shines. When the class is doing something well, identify it. When correction is needed, provide it, coupled with a tailored opportunity to apply it correctly and repeatedly.

A Trans-Disciplinary Lesson

A concept that is shared by all of these fields, though they may use different terminology, is that of alignment. One of the key roles played by leadership, regardless of context, is ensuring the alignment of the people, processes, and culture with the values and mission of the larger organization. In essence, alignment is when every element is pushing or pulling in the same direction.

Since teaching is a form of leadership, this concept applies in much the same way. Student engagement is such a crucial metric of a successful lesson in part because it correlates with alignment. Any veteran teacher will know the outsized effect a single unengaged student can have on a group. This is because they are pulling in a different direction.

There is, however, another kind of alignment with which educators must be concerned: alignment across structural levels. It can be visualized in this way:

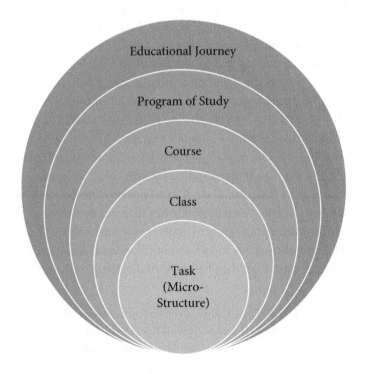

Tasks are the building blocks of classes, which combine to make courses, which make up a program of study, which, in turn, contributes to an individual's educational journey. The ideas in this book focus on micro-structures, the smallest level, which shape and guide student actions and interactions during a lesson. Of course, educators need to be aware of every one of these levels, monitoring and contributing to their alignment all the way from learning tasks to learning journey. However, during the times when a teacher is actively engaged in teaching a lesson, the teacher's attention is most effective when focused on the first two levels. This does not mean to ignore the larger levels, but that, when teaching, the learning tasks and class objectives take center stage.

Planning a lesson supported by FERM structures begins with the question "What will this group of learners be able to do by the end of the class?" If you struggle to answer this question, try contextualizing it by adding "...so that they will move closer to meeting the objectives of the course?" Presumably, the course objectives will already be aligned with the mission of the program and the encompassing purpose of education as a journey. Reflecting on these occasionally is a valuable practice.

Once you have identified an objective for the class, check whether it is *specific, measurable, achievable, relevant,* and *timely* (or SMART). "They will be better at asking follow-up questions" satisfies only a few of these. "They will reliably be able to ask open-ended follow-up questions in response to any statement whose topic they are familiar with" satisfies more of them, especially if being able to ask such follow-up questions fits sensibly into a larger framework of skills being developed in service of reaching an orienting goal. "What will students be able to do by the end of class?" is a guiding question, providing both a litmus test for micro-structures you are considering and a compass to direct you when real-time adaptations are required.

As the above diagram represents, the class you create is its own structure and should be carefully designed to facilitate some outcome within a larger framework. One of the defining characteristics of micro-structures is their combinability. First, identify what you want to accomplish. Then, build a flexible structure to get you there using individually solid but collectively synergistic micro-structures. This is how systems thinking can be applied to lesson design. In contrast, an activity-based approach to lesson design consists of the teacher looking at the material to be covered and identifying the "best" activity for each portion of that material. This is like building a team by throwing together the best players for each position: it is rarely successful because the relationships between the parts and the likelihood that they will work well *together* is left to chance. In all likelihood, what you end up with is a series of stand-alone activities. This does not qualify as a structurally sound class. Micro-structures, on the other hand, are building blocks designed to fit together into a cohesive whole that, itself, is part of a larger project.

Summary and Conclusion

As you can tell from this chapter, FERM structures are founded upon something more than the typical SLA fare. While in keeping with the best principles from this field (lessons are student centered, communication is meaning focused and rich in feedback), this approach also incorporates valuable lessons from other disciplines with a rich history of thought and practice. Organizational development presents the class as a learning team with the teacher acting as a leader responsible for developing its confidence and liberating its intelligence. Military training methods keep the focus on fundamentals, realism, and repetition by dividing up complex skills into practicable components that can be slowly evolved and combined to provide the exact challenge required for the next stage of development. From the field of coaching, we get the criteria to cultivate psychological safety so that students will feel safe enough to make the best effort of which they are capable. All four of these disciplines come together into a single approach that helps us teach, lead, train, and coach the learners in our classroom so that they develop the knowledge and skills they need.

The next section of this book presents a collection of FERM structures that, essentially, are examples of how this set of principles can be applied. Treating them as discrete tasks will refresh your current teaching practice, but treating them as a cohesive system will transform how you teach.

Section 2

HOW TO USE STRUCTURE-BASED TEACHING

Chapter 4

50 FERM STRUCTURES

This section contains 50 FERM structures that you can take and adapt to suit your lessons. They are arranged in alphabetical order. For each structure, you will find five pieces of information to help you decide which ones might work best in your lesson.

1. A Graphic Illustration

This condenses the main patterns of interaction into a simple visual representation that illustrates how the structure works. Once you are familiar with the structures, a quick glance at the image should remind you what is involved.

2. Learning Tasks

Here are some common learning tasks for which this structure is particularly well-suited. For example, some of the FERM structures work well with a reading passage, others work well for learning vocabulary or brainstorming.

If you are incorporating the FERM approach with a course that uses a set textbook, this section will help you choose appropriate structures to use with the textbook content.

The main task categories are:

- warmer
- predicting
- reading
- vocabulary learning
- comprehension check
- brainstorming
- discussion
- critical reflection
- problem solving

- expressing an opinion
- grammar practice
- listening

3. Description

This is a written description of the structure, often with examples of how it might work practically.

4. Variations

Some ways to adapt or tweak the structure to work in different ways are suggested here.

5. Combinations

Here you will find some other FERM structures that work particularly well with this one, either before or after, or even concurrently.

1. 1-by-1

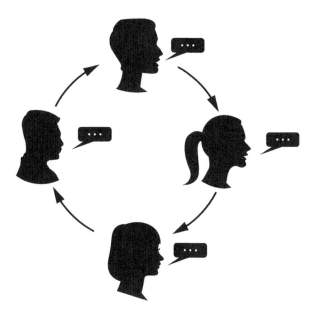

Learning tasks

Vocabulary learning   Grammar practice

Description

1-by-1 is the most straightforward structure in terms of design—so much so, in fact, that the authors discussed whether to include it at all in this manual. It made the cut for a few reasons:

- It is often appropriate for the first application of new content.
- It is the easiest and most versatile structure for connecting other, more involved structures.
- It has many useful evolutions.

1-by-1 consists of having the learners perform an act sequentially. That is, one learner goes first, followed by the next and then the next. It is best done in groups of two to five. Sounds simple, right? Take note of the variations below.

Variations

1. *One word*: Each learner responds with one word. For example, "Name an activity that elderly people often do on the weekend." (gardening, walking, reading…)
2. *One sentence*: Each learner makes a sentence that uses a vocabulary word taken from a list.
3. *Half sentences*: The learner stops midway through a sentence, determined by the lesson topic or target grammar, and the next student completes the sentence.
4. *Build a sentence*: The first learner says the first word of a sentence and each subsequent learner says a single word that continues the sentence until they are able to reach a successful completion. They can be asked to use target vocabulary in this sentence.
5. *Build a story*: The first learner uses a vocabulary word to make a sentence or two to begin a story. The next learner uses a different vocabulary word and continues the story. The goal for the story can be to explore a theme, to retell a reading passage, to use up a list of vocabulary items, or something else.
6. *UNO*: The first learner makes a sentence that incorporates the target vocabulary and grammar. The next student repeats the sentence but changes either (a) the vocabulary or (b) the grammar. For example, first learner: "The bank is next to the bookstore." Second learner: "The bank is opposite the bookstore." Third learner: "The bus stop is opposite the bookstore."

Combinations

Picture Vocab   Expanding Sentences

An Additional Note about 1-by-1

Please do not allow the apparent simplicity of this structure to convince you it can be overlooked. Its simplicity also makes it the most flexible of the structures with an array of variations, evolutions, and combinations available to it.

1-by-1 can be thought of as the homebase structure. It is always a good place to start because it can be appropriately tailored for learners who are just starting to grapple with a new list of vocabulary words or a tricky grammar point. It also serves as a good second step since it can be levelled up in a gradual manner. Once the learners have developed some familiarity and fluency with the target language, they can be challenged with another structure.

1-by-1 is also a place to which you can return regularly. Learners who are working with a complex structure that relies on creativity and a broad knowledge base can be brought back to *1-by-1* to reestablish their focus on the core content of the lesson. This kind of spaced and varied practice, in which you work on something for a short time, change focus, and then come back to the first point of focus, supports increased learning efficiency. The same can be said of interleaving, wherein the style of engagement with the content is altered. Learning happens when the process of forgetting is repeatedly interrupted. Spaced, varied, and interleaved styles of practice are effective for learning because they allow the process of forgetting to begin, only to then step in and signal that the target content is once again required and cannot be forgotten. Using *1-by-1* as a homebase allows the teacher to easily satisfy these criteria of efficient practice.

2. 1-2-4 All

Learning tasks

Discussion   Comprehension check   Problem solving

Description

First, students are given a prompt or a question that they try to answer on their own. After a prescribed amount of time, they share their idea(s) in a pair. Then, two pairs join to make a group of four. The goal of each subsequent stage is to compare and combine answers. Once time is up for the groups of four, each group shares their answers or ideas with the whole class. Thus, the number of people interacting moves from one, to two, to four, to all.

The "all" stage can be managed in several ways, such as a presentation, as something written on a shared board, as something shared in newly formed groups, etc. Almost any kind of question works with this structure.

Variations

1. For lower ability levels, you might ask them to make a list of words related to a topic.
2. For higher ability levels, you can ask them to define an abstract concept or identify possible solutions to a problem.
3. This also works well with any common exercise or learning task taken from a coursebook.
4. *Online:* Starting in breakout rooms, students can work alone, then with a partner by chat, then with their whole room. A summary of their ideas can be shared verbally or written in the class chat.

Combinations

Diamond 9   *R-R-R*

3. 50/50 Questions

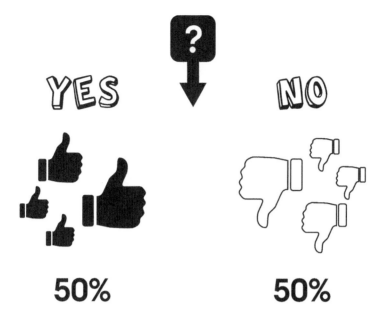

Learning tasks

Predicting   Critical reflection

Description

Learners formulate a dichotomous question (or set of questions) that they believe half of the class will answer one way and the other half the other way. The answers to these questions often take the form of yes/no, agree/disagree, or option one/ option two. The formulation of the questions can be done individually, in pairs, or in small groups.

> Examples:
> *Did you have fruit for breakfast this morning?*
> *The death penalty should be abolished. Do you agree?*
> *Is it better for children to play sports or learn a musical instrument?*

Students then ask each other the questions in order to test whether, in fact, the answers are split 50/50. Interactions can be managed in a structured way (rotating lines) or unstructured (free mingling). After each question has been asked and answered several times, you can ask the students to determine which question produced a response split closest to 50/50. That question can then be used in a following structure.

Variations

1. The ratio can be changed; for example, a 75/25 question.
2. *Online:* Students can decide their questions individually, then ask them in breakout rooms.

Combinations

R-R-R   *Devil vs. Angel*   *Hot Seat*

4. 50/50 Quiz

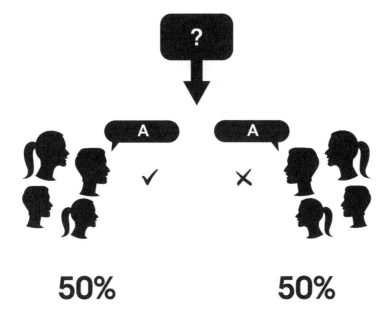

Learning tasks

Predicting   Critical reflection

Description

Learners make quiz questions that they think only half of the class will answer correctly. The questions can be about material that was covered in class, in which case it is a good way to review and consolidate learning. Alternatively, questions can be about a topic yet to be covered, in which case it allows the teacher to check current understanding. Or, of course, questions can be about anything the students choose. The 50/50 requirement means that questions cannot be too difficult, nor too easy.

After deciding their questions and making sure they have the correct answers, the learners ask around the class.

After asking around, the hardest question, the easiest question, or the question that came closest to obtaining half correct answers can be identified and used for the next structure. Alternatively, the learners can summarize the right answers they gave and the new things they learned.

Variations

1. The percentages can be adjusted. For example: 25/75 (25% correct, 75% incorrect), or 80/20 (80% correct, 20% incorrect)
2. Partners can be instructed to ask a counter-question before giving their answer, and questioners can be instructed to provide the correct answers (or not) once an attempt has been made.

Combinations

Di/Con/It   Co-op Remembering

5. A & Q

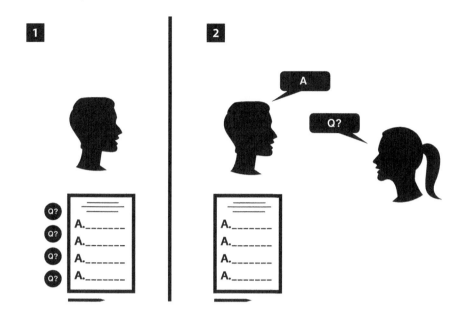

Learning tasks

Warmer   Discussion

Description

The learners answer a question or set of questions. They share their answer(s) with a partner who tries to guess the question.

If there is a set of common questions, then the partner listens carefully to the answer and chooses which question from the list was answered. Alternatively, if the question is one that the partner has never seen, they have to listen carefully and consider what the question could be.

As a lead-in, this structure prepares the groundwork for other structures that task learners with guessing the opinions of their classmates. Examples are *50/50 Questions*, *Spectrum Questions*, and *Unique Questions*. You can also lead in to structures like *Co-op Remembering*.

As a follow-up, it works well after structures that produce a set of questions.

Variations

1. Learners can be given a set of questions prepared by the teacher, or from the textbook, that are related to the content of the unit being studied.

2. Learners can think up their own questions independently, or in a group, and write down the answers to those.

Combinations

Spectrum Questions   *Unique Questions*

6. Ask, Answer, Add

Learning tasks

Discussion   Expressing an opinion

Description

The first learner answers an initial question of some type. This can be short and simple, or a planned and written response. The partner then asks a follow-up question about that answer, to which the first learner responds.

Learners then find a new partner. This time, in answer to the same initial question, the learner gives their initial answer but adds the extra information given in answer to the first partner's follow-up question. The new partner must now ask a different follow-up question.

Learners then change partners, and the task is repeated. Each time, the answer gets longer and longer. This continues for a certain number of rounds, or a set time.

Example sequence:

Round One	Round Two (with a new partner)	Round Three (with a new partner)
A: What did you do last weekend? B: I went to Tokyo. A: (*Follow-up question*). Who did you go with? B: I went with my sister.	C: What did you do last weekend? B: I went to Tokyo with my sister. C: (*Follow-up question*). Why? B: We went to visit our grandmother.	D: What did you do last weekend? B: I went to Tokyo with my sister. We wanted to see our grandmother. D: (*Follow-up question*). How often…? (etc.)

Variations

Adding a time limit to the initial answer will encourage the learners to pack more information into their response, while at the same time promoting efficiency and automaticity. Alternatively, you might limit the initial answer to one sentence.

Combinations

R-R-R   *Quote Search*   *Teach It to Me*

7. Attention Up Front

Learning tasks

Explicit instruction

Description

This is the only structure that is designed for a one-way flow of information from the teacher to the learners. It's used any time explicit instruction is called for, such as imparting some knowledge or training students in a skill. In other words, use this structure whenever you want to "teach" something.

It's very simple. Just announce, "Attention up front" and make sure that all the learners are focused on you. Then, present one of the language points from the goals of that lesson.

This can be done *before* a structure, so that learners can then practice that language. It can also be done *after* a structure, in order to correct some common errors that were made. It can even be done *during* a structure, when you notice that learners are struggling with some aspect of the language.

Variations

1. The mode of instruction can vary, such as on a whiteboard, on a screen, or from a coursebook.
2. Rather than teacher instruction, you can divide up the target language between groups of learners, and each group can be tasked with presenting that point to the rest of the class.

Combinations

Works well with every other structure

8. Best Case, Worst Case

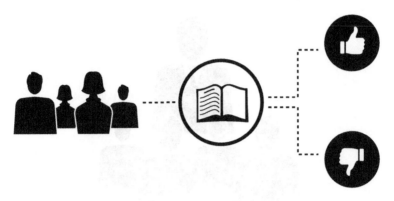

Learning tasks

Critical reflection   Discussion

Description

In response to a situation of some kind, the learners identify what the best- and worst-case outcomes are. They can develop and present these in any way that fits the lesson.

For example, if the lesson topic is "daily routines," you can ask, "If you got up at 4 am every day, what is the best [or worst] thing that could happen?"

If the lesson topic is being environmentally friendly, you can ask, "If the government banned the use of all cars, what is the best [or worst] thing that could happen?"

Variations

1. This could also take the form of a debate. In small groups, or as a whole class, half the learners argue that the best case is more likely to happen, while the other half argue that the worst case is more likely.
2. The debate could also focus on whether or not to take a certain action given the best and worst case scenarios that could result.

Combinations

50/50 Questions   *Devil vs. Angel*

9. Cameraman Interview

Learning tasks

Predicting   Warmer

Description

Choose a picture from the textbook, or else find a picture online or from another source that is related to the topic currently being studied. In pairs, one learner plays the role of the cameraman—they imagine that they were the one that took this photo. The other learner plays the role of an interviewer. They ask questions such as:

- Where did you take this picture?
- When was it taken?
- How did you feel?
- What happened before you took it?
- What happened after you took it?
- Who is the person in the background?
- etc.

Variations

1. Instead of using a picture from the textbook or the teacher, learners could search online for a picture, according to the topic being studied.
2. Learners could use a photo in their smartphone album that they themselves have actually taken.

Combinations

Picture Vocab   Hot Seat

10. Choose and Use

Learning tasks

Vocabulary learning   Comprehension check

Description

The first learner chooses a vocabulary word that the second learner uses in a sentence. The second learner then chooses the next word. The vocabulary list can come from whatever is currently being studied in the unit. Phrases or grammar points can be used instead of vocabulary words.

Variations

1. This task can be done in pairs. Alternatively, learners can do it in a group of three to four by going round a circle.
2. Additional challenge can be added in a group by having two learners make two different sentences using the chosen word.

Combinations

Cold Call   *Word Associations*   *Partner Quiz*

11. Collecting Questions

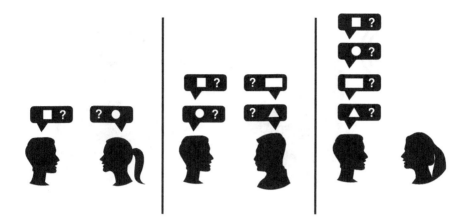

Learning tasks

Discussion   Comprehension check

Description

Each learner begins with a single original question that they have come up with themselves. They make pairs and pose that question to their partner. The learners need to remember the question that their partner asked so that, added to their own question, they now have a total of two questions.

Then they find a new partner. This time they must ask their original question, plus the question asked by their first partner. They also answer two questions, which they must also remember, so that now they have a total of four questions.

Then learners get a new partner, and the process continues. Each time, they try and ask all of the questions they have answered so far.

Variations

Instead of collecting questions, the learners can collect answers. In this case, they will ask their question and then recount the answers they have gotten so far, before asking, "How about you?"

Combinations

Unique Questions   Co-op Remembering

12. Co-op Listening

Learning tasks

Listening   Comprehension check

Description

Learners work in pairs or groups. One learner is responsible for listening and remembering, the other for listening and taking notes. In the case of groups, split them into those who remember and those who take notes. The instructor then talks about or reads something pertinent to the topic of the class. Alternatively, you can use audio from the textbook, a video, or a podcast. The learners do their best to listen and remember or listen and note what they hear.

Afterwards, they share what they remembered and noted, trying to reconstruct as much of it as they can. You can also have them switch roles halfway through. The instructor can then share a full script with the learners (or not) depending on which structure is done next.

Variations

This can be done in a group of three, with one learner reading the passage and two learners engaging in listening (one remembering and one note-taking). Once finished, the two listeners can check their answers with the reader.

Online: When working with large groups, it is a good idea to prepare breakout rooms, share the passage they are trying to remember, then open the breakout rooms. This allows for the smoothest transition from listening to cooperatively remembering.

Combinations

Predict the Material   *Fact or Fiction*   *Question Storming*

13. Co-op Remembering

Learning tasks

Critical reflection   Comprehension check

Description

Learners work in pairs or groups to remember as much as they can of something that was previously presented. This can be an image flashed on the screen, a passage read by the teacher, or a video. It can also be a follow-up structure to others like *R-R-R* or *Quote Search*, in which you ask the groups to remember the ideas and opinions shared by other students. Such follow-up uses add a level of difficulty to the structure since each member will have been exposed to different information and, thus, cannot rely on others to remember.

As a lead-in structure, *Co-op Remembering* can be used to develop a sense of the class before doing *50/50 Questions* or *Spectrum Questions*. If you have learners cooperatively remember a story (e.g., Cinderella), you could follow up with *1-by-1: Build a Story*, using the remembered one as a template.

This is also a handy structure to use in the beginning of each class by asking the students to recall what was covered last time.

Variations

When in groups, each learner could be given a specific set of details to remember, such as names, dates, advantages, disadvantages, etc.

Combinations

R-R-R   *Quote Search*   *50/50 Questions*   *1-by-1: Build a Story*

14. Creative Comparisons

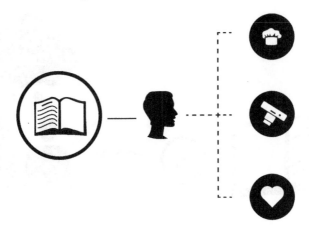

Learning tasks

Warmer   Critical reflection

Description

The learners are tasked with making a sentence that makes a comparison to some prompt and gives supporting reasons. For example, the prompt "getting angry" might produce the sentence "Getting angry is like eating ice-cream because it feels good while you do it, but can also make a mess." Learners can then share and react.

Variations

1. Learners can also interview one another about their comparisons, asking questions like, "what kind of ice-cream is it?" and "what else can you tell me about the ice-cream?"
2. Learners can be provided with two words or ideas, and then try to find as many similarities as they can between them. For example, "a penguin and a baby," "a computer and a hammer," or "the President and a pencil."

Combinations

Self-Sorting   Co-op Remembering

15. Di/Con/It

1. **Di**verge 2. **Con**verge 3. **It**erate

Learning tasks

Discussion   Problem solving

Description

"Di" stands for diverge, "Con" for converge, and "It" for iterate. This structure is a stripped-down design thinking process. It starts with a question that does not have a single correct answer. The learners then try to formulate a high-quality answer by going through three stages.

First, they *diverge* by recording as many possible answers as they can without judging the merits of any. The goal is quantity, not quality. Second, they *converge* by discussing which of their answers is the most attractive. Finally, they *iterate* by trying to improve the answer they settled on.

For example, the question may be: "What is the best after-school activity for children?"

1. *Diverge answers*: swimming, music lessons, soccer, playing in a park, computer games, etc.
2. *Converge answer*: A music lesson is the best activity, because it helps the brain develop.
3. *Iterate answer*: Playing a guitar twice a week is best, as long as the child has free time on other days.

This process is simple but powerful, training learners to suspend judgment during ideation, to cooperatively evaluate their options, and to synthesize the desirable aspects of multiple ideas.

Variations

Each group could write down their most attractive idea after the second stage (converge) and then swap papers with another group. The other group could then engage in the third stage (iterate).

Combinations

Speedy Summaries   *Best Case, Worst Case*

16. Devil vs. Angel

Learning tasks

Critical reflection   Expressing an opinion

Description

First, some question or proposition is identified. This could be a topic for debate, such as "Smartphones should be banned in high school," or a binary question, such as "Are there some situations in which it's OK to cheat on a test?"

In groups of three to five, learners are divided into three roles: listener, supporter, and refuter. The listener(s) listens to the arguments of the supporter(s) and refuter(s) for a set amount of time. After that, the listener(s) decides who was more convincing, explains why, and answers any follow-up questions.

You can then change roles and repeat with a different (or the same) question or proposition.

The name *Devil vs. Angel* comes from the trope that we each have a devil and an angel on our shoulders, arguing different points. The supporter(s) and refuter(s) need not respect one another's speaking time. They can try to interrupt, talk over, etc.

Variations

1. Instead of the speakers working at odds, they can work as a pair to present one side of the issue for a set amount of time. Then, they switch and present the other side. The listener then decides which presentation was more convincing.

2. You can also have the listener share their opinion before starting. The supporter and refuter can then behave as normal, or they can act as a team trying to change the listener's mind.

Combinations

Di/Con/It   *Writing Storm*   *Writing Chain*

17. Diamond 9

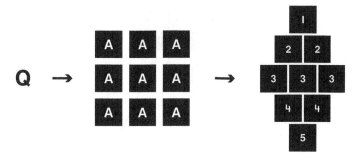

Learning tasks

Critical reflection   Discussion

Description

Begin with a question (or a prompt) that permits multiple answers (or opinions). Learners then identify nine different answers to the question. Ideally, this would be done on sticky notes or cards that could be moved around. But, in a pinch, a piece of paper or whiteboard will work.

The next step is to organize these answers according to their quality or appeal by placing or rewriting them in the shape of a diamond: the best answer on top, two answers in the second row, three in the middle row, two in the fourth, and the least attractive answer at the bottom.

Once finished, learners take a note or a photo on their smartphone, make new groups, and explain their diamond to the new group.

Variations

1. As an extension, groups could exchange answer cards and make a new diamond using the other group's answers.
2. Each group could be given a different question. Then, students could visit the completed diamonds of other groups and guess what question they were answering.
3. *Online:* In lieu of a physical medium, a digital one could be used. This may be your preferred medium, even when conducting face-to-face classes, as it allows groups to easily view each other's diamonds.

Combinations

Unique Questions   Co-op Remembering

18. Different Questions, Same Answer

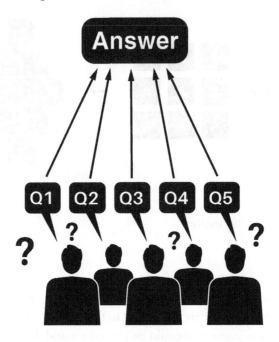

Learning tasks

Vocabulary learning

Description

Learners identify as many questions as they can that will all have the same answer. For example, given the answer "orange" they could write questions like:

What color is a mix of red and yellow?

What is a fruit you can squeeze to get juice?

The target word can be a vocabulary word to review, randomly chosen by another team, or related to the content being covered. The questions can then be used with new partners who can guess the word if they don't already know it.

Alternatively, the structure can be used with non-vocabulary words to stress a grammar point related to questions. For example, "The answer is summer. Make as many questions as you can that start with "which."

Which season is the hottest?

Which season is good for going to the beach?

Variations

1. Learners can create cloze versions of the questions. For example:

The answer is "orange." The question is "What color is a _____ of red and yellow?"

2. Instead of a single word, the answer could be a phrase. For example, "Healthy eating habits" or "Free internet connection."

3. *Online:* The teacher can broadcast answers to students in breakout rooms who then employ a 1-by-1 structure to take turns identifying questions.

Combinations

1-2-4 All   *List and Switch*   *Partner Quiz*   *Unique Questions*

19. Every Open-Ended Question

Learning tasks

Comprehension check   Reading   Listening

Description

Individuals, pairs, or groups are tasked with formulating six questions—one each starting with *who, what, when, where, why,* and *how.* The prompt for these questions can be anything (e.g., a picture, a passage of text, a theme).

Variations

1. Learners can work in pairs or groups, each of which is given a question word (or two): *who, what, when, where, why,* and *how.* They think of as many questions as they can using their assigned question word(s).
2. Learners write down the answers to questions beginning with *who, what, when, where, why,* and *how.* They then swap their answers and try to work out what the questions were.

Combinations

Unique Questions   Hot Seat   Listen In

20. Expanding Sentences

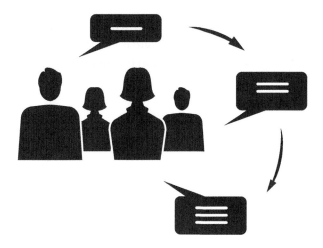

Learning tasks

Vocabulary learning   Grammar practice

Description

Learners begin with a simple sentence that is then repeatedly built upon. The first learner begins by answering a question, using a vocabulary word, etc. The second learner then repeats the first sentence but adds something to it. The third learner repeats that but adds something again to make it even longer.

This structure works particularly well with relative clauses (e.g., "I saw a man who was wearing a hat, which was made from cotton, that came from…"), but it can be done with conjunctive adverbs like "but," "therefore," etc., or with adjectives and adverbs. Anything you can add to a sentence to make it longer should work.

One thing to avoid, however, is allowing the learners to freely use "and." They should be fashioning an ever longer sentence, not reciting a list. Also, students should be encouraged to correct any errors in the sentence as they go. Doing so may help them uncover points and formulations they are unsure about. Addressing these is a good way to follow up on the structure.

The students should keep going until the sentence becomes too long and someone forgets it, they have used all the vocab words, or some other limitation is reached.

Variations

1. Rather than correcting errors in the sentence, a rule can be made that the sentence resets and begins again if there is an error.
2. Transition words such as "because" can be limited to single use only.

Combinations

1-by-1   Choose and Use

21. Expert Interview

Reporter   **Expert**

Learning tasks

Discussion   Expressing an opinion

Description

One learner acts as an expert on a topic, answering all questions posed by their partner, who acts as a reporter. The actual degree of expertise possessed by the learner is of no importance. The "expert" responds to any and all questions with an authoritative answer. Blatantly wrong and/or silly answers are to be encouraged.

Variations

1. If done before a unit of study, this can be used to elicit how much students know (or think they know) about the topic before the unit commences.
2. If done at the end of a unit, it can be used to see how much students have learned. However, students should be reminded that even if they don't know the "real" answer, they should give a confident reply. In this way, the usual anxiety that comes with being tested on a unit is greatly reduced.
3. The teacher can also present learners with an absurd topic of expertise (e.g., underwater gardening) and put the emphasis on a grammar point or set of vocabulary words to be used in the questions asked and/or answers given.

Combinations

Hot Seat   Picture Role Play

22. Fact Checkers

Learning tasks

Grammar practice   Comprehension check

Description

One learner has a reading passage in which the grammar and content are correct. Before reading it aloud, they change something (or several things) about the passage to make it incorrect. Their partner is tasked with identifying the mistakes.

This structure can be used to reinforce vocabulary, grammar, or other content by changing the kind of errors made by the readers. The speed of the reading, number and severity of the errors, and the option to correct the mistakes are all ways the structure can be adjusted.

Variations

1. Instead of using a reading passage, the speaker can read from a transcript of a listening passage that the learners have previously been exposed to.
2. The listener can be tasked with counting the mistakes, stopping and correcting the speaker, or looking at the passage and circling everything that is different from what they heard.

Combinations

R-R-R   *Expert Interview*

23. Fact or Fiction

Learning tasks

Comprehension check   Critical reflection

Description

In a pair or in a group, one learner makes a series of statements. The other learner(s) judge whether each statement is fact or fiction (you could also say "truth" or "lie"). Learners can be asked to come up with any number of statements. For example, two statements of fact and one of fiction, or five statements of fact and five of fiction. Likewise, their partners can be asked to identify one or all of the facts or fictions.

There are many sources from which these statements could come. For example:
1. *Written text.* Learners form statements based on a text that the other student has (or hasn't) read.
2. *Picture.* Statements are formed about the content of a picture, such as the location of objects or the actions of people.
3. *Infographic, graph, or pie chart.* Some kind of statistical information displayed visually can serve as a source for statements.
4. *Personal experience.* Learners make statements about themselves, such as things they did in high school or how they spent the weekend.

Variations

This works particularly well at the beginning of a course as a get-to-know-you activity. In this variation, students make three statements about themselves, two of which are true and one of which is a lie. Follow-up questions can be encouraged to add layers to the structure. These allow the guessing students to interrogate the speaker before they choose the lie(s), putting more creative pressure on the author of the statements.

Combinations

Hot Seat   R-R-R

24. Hot Seat

Learning tasks

Expressing an opinion   Discussion

Description

Learners are in groups of three to five people. One learner is in the "Hot Seat," which means the other students bombard that person with questions. Because the questioners are in a group, they have some time to think, so should always be ready with a good follow-up question.

For the questioners, the emphasis is on listening comprehension and asking quality follow-up questions. For the learner in the hot seat, the emphasis is on fluency, as they will need to quickly respond to follow-up questions. The *Hot Seat* goes for a set amount of time before rotating to the next learner. *Hot Seat* helps the learners to better understand their own opinions and experiences and those of their group.

Variations

1. The learner being interviewed can take on the character of someone in a coursebook. This could be a character from a sample conversational dialogue or someone who is described in a reading passage.
2. The questioners can be limited in various ways, such as asking only follow-up questions or only open-ended questions.
3. The structure can also be flipped, so that one person interviews the rest. This structure is called a *Panel Interview*.

Combinations

Unique Questions   *50/50 Questions*

25. Imaginary Friend

Learning tasks

Discussion   Grammar practice

Description

Learners are given a picture of someone they do not know. A good way to provide this is to use thispersondoesnotexist.com, a website that uses AI to generate faces of people who do not actually exist. Since none of the people are real, learners are likely to feel greater license to be creative.

These pictures are used to inspire subsequent interactions based around that lesson's topic or that employ particular grammar points or vocabulary for review. For example, a learner could:

- describe and answer questions about that person's schedule
- tell a story from that person's life
- describe that person's lifestyle, personality, and job
- use the past perfect to explain what that person did before coming to school
- use the third conditional to express that person's regrets in life

Basically, this structure can combine with any language exercise or drill by having students do that exercise through the lens of an imaginary friend.

Variations

Instead of using the website mentioned above, you could choose a random person from a photo in your textbook. Alternatively, download a selection of random pictures from an internet image search and print them out before class.

Combinations

R-R-R   *Hot Seat*   *1-by-1: Build a Story*

26. List and Switch

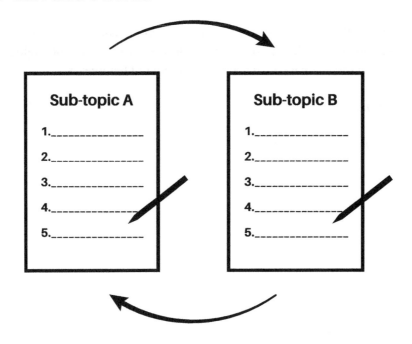

Learning tasks

Brainstorming   Critical reflection

Description

First, the class is broken up into groups according to sub-topics. Each group has one piece of paper and works together to create a list of answers. Then, after a set amount of time, or a set number of ideas have been recorded, the groups switch papers (and also topics) and try to add to the lists they receive.

For example: On the topic of "study abroad," one sub-topic could be the advantages of study abroad and the other sub-topic could be the disadvantages of study abroad. One group would list the advantages, another group would list the disadvantages. After three minutes, they would switch papers and try to add to the previous group's ideas.

List and Switch need not be limited to binary sub-topics. If, for example, the topic was "wellbeing," you might make three groups with the sub-topics "psychological wellbeing," "physical wellbeing," and "social wellbeing." You could then rotate twice so each group has a chance at each sub-topic.

Variations

1. Sub-topics can be assigned to individuals instead of groups. In this case, rather than one sheet of paper per group, there is one sheet of paper per student. The papers are rotated within the group.
2. You can have pairs of individuals (or groups) switch lists three or four times, or even compare lists that they themselves haven't written.
3. *Online:* Instead of papers, you can use an online collaborative platform that allows multiple users to read and edit a single document.

Combinations

Teach It to Me   *Picture Vocab*   *Writing Storm*

27. Listen In

Learning tasks

Discussion   Critical reflection

Description

In groups of three or four, two learners begin as the speakers while the others act as listeners. The speakers talk for a predetermined length of time about some topic. After this time is up, they turn to the listeners who, based on what they heard, ask follow-up questions to the speakers.

This can be repeated for rounds or simply done once. In groups of three, one learner listens and then asks questions to both speakers. In groups of four, each speaker gets their own dedicated listener.

Variations

1. Instead of having listeners ask follow-up questions to the speakers, the listeners can:
    a. summarize or paraphrase what they heard
    b. provide feedback, agreeing or disagreeing with what was said
    c. suggest the next topic for discussion
2. For the purpose of vocabulary learning, speakers can be tasked with using as many of the vocabulary words as they can. The listeners' job is to keep track of how many words are used in the discussion. When all the words have been used, listener and speaker roles can be reversed.

Combinations

Predict the Material   Teach It to Me

(This can be combined with almost all the structures by having listeners listen in to the people who are engaged in the structure.)

28. Need to Know

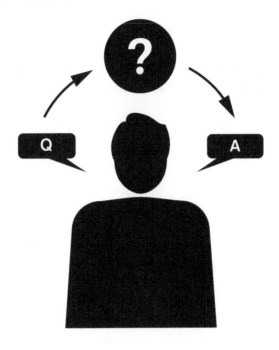

Learning tasks

Critical reflection   Problem solving

Description

First, learners are given a question. This can be provided by the teacher, it can come from a unit in the textbook, or, preferably, it can be determined by the learners themselves. Most questions produced by other structures that end with the learners having formulated a question (e.g., *50/50 Questions*, *Spectrum Questions*) should be suitable. You can also have learners come up with these initial questions on the fly.

Then, learners are tasked with identifying questions they would need answered *before* they can answer the initial question. A question like, "What job do you want to have in the future?" might inspire a learner to respond with, "Where will I be living? Will I have a family? What year are we talking about?" and so on.

The number of *Need to Know* questions can be decided by the teacher, as can whether the partners are tasked with answering these questions.

Variations

For an added challenge, students could be asked to make five *who, what, when, why,* and *where Need to Know* questions.

Combinations

50/50 Questions   *Spectrum Questions*

29. Pair Dictation

Learning tasks

Reading   Listening

Description

Start with some text. One learner reads the passage while their partner listens and takes notes. The reading should be smooth and done at a natural speed. Material should not be repeated. If the passage is particularly long, roles can be switched halfway through.

At the end of the passage, put away the material so that it cannot be seen. The learners then work together to reconstruct as much of it as they can.

This structure can be evolved by having the teacher ask comprehension questions to check understanding. Alternatively, you can ask pairs to compare their final products.

Be sure to remind students that the goal is not to memorize and repeat verbatim the content of the passage. Rather, the goal is synthesis and paraphrasing. Learners can express the main ideas in the text in their own words and phrases.

Variations

1. Each group can be given a different passage from a longer text. After engaging in the task, members from different groups come together and try to put their final summaries in a logical order.
2. The writing student can be asked to take notes in the form of a mind map, story board, or other alternative method.

Combinations

Predict the Material   Ask, Answer, Add

30. Partner Quiz

Learning tasks

Comprehension check   Critical reflection

Description

Learners work in pairs. They are both exposed in some way to the same content. This may mean they both look at the same picture or infographic. It may mean they listen to the same dialogue or skim the same reading section. Then, one learner removes their access to the content (e.g., closes their book, turns their back to the board, etc.). Their partner uses the content to ask questions, checking what they can remember.

Changing the style of questions permitted is an easy way to scale the demands of this structure. For example, telling the quiz givers to ask "what" questions about a reading passage, or to refrain from reading any of the passage as part of their question, will lead to both learners engaging meaningfully with the text.

Variations

This can also be done as a game, in a group of three to four learners. One learner is the "Quiz Master," and the other learners compete against each other to answer the questions correctly.

Combinations

A & Q   *50/50 Questions*

31. Picture Role Play

Learning tasks

Predicting   Warmer

Description

Learners are provided with a picture from a coursebook, or one supplied by the teacher, that has at least two people in it. The learners then take the role of the people in the picture. Ask them to consider what each person's personality may be, the reason why that person is in this situation, and their primary motivation. Learners role play the situation for a set time limit, engaging in dialogue.

Variations

1. To increase the challenge and inspire creativity, learners could role play a dialogue between a person and an object in the picture (e.g., a man and his sandwich) or an animal (e.g., an elderly woman and her cat).
2. Instead of doing a spoken role play, students can work together to write a dialogue between two people (or objects) in the picture.
3. In a subsequent structure, learners can work in new pairs to compare the role plays they enacted. Doing multiple role plays for a single picture is also a way to challenge the learners' creativity.
4. Instead of a picture, characters can be taken from a reading or listening passage.

Combinations

Picture Vocab   Hot Seat

32. Picture Vocab

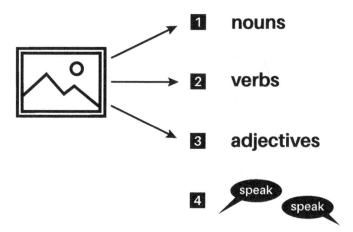

Learning tasks

Predicting   Vocabulary learning

Description

Learners are presented with a visual prompt (a photograph, an illustration, a short video, etc.). The prompt can be taken from a coursebook or found through an online image search. The task is to list words that describe that piece of visual media.

In order to focus ideas more, you can break it down by having learners first list nouns only, next verbs, and then adjectives. Once they have a list of useful words, the final task is to talk freely about the image, giving their thoughts, opinions, and ideas.

Variations

1. This can be conducted as a team game, with points awarded for the number of words written down.
2. The visual prompt can be taken away and the learners asked to produce vocabulary or descriptions from memory.
3. This can also be done as a quiz with students answering questions or responding with "true" or "false" to their partners' descriptions. After they both examine the image, one student closes their book, and their partner looks at the image and makes a statement, such as "The girl eating ice-cream has curly hair." From memory, the first student declares "true" or "false."

Combinations

1-by-1: One Sentence   Picture Role Play   List and Switch

33. Predict the Material

Next topic

Learning tasks

Predicting   Reading   Listening

Description

This is useful for any time you want the learners to make a prediction about what they are about to do or learn. You can give them the title or topic of the next unit and ask them what vocabulary they think it includes or which skills it covers. Alternatively, you can have them read the title of an article or look at a photo in a textbook unit and predict its contents.

Asking for predictions is a simple, effective way to increase engagement and retention.

Variations

1. This can be used before structures like *R-R-R* by having learners predict what their partners are going to say.
2. When predicting a listening task, it can be performed as a role play. For example, before listening to a dialogue, you can explain the characters and the situation of the dialogue, and then have learners role play how they think the conversation might take place.
3. This structure can be used with a reading or listening comprehension task in your textbook. Have the students read and answer the comprehension questions *before* they read the passage or listen to the audio. Then, they can read or listen to the text to check their predictions.

Combinations

1-2-4 All   List and Switch

34. Quote Search

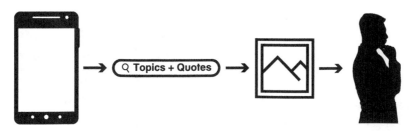

Learning tasks

Warmer　　　Expressing an opinion

Description

(Note: As described here, this structure requires each learner to have internet access. Smartphones are a good option if available. If this is not an option, enterprising teachers could compile a list of quotes from which the learners would be able to choose.)

Learners are first tasked with finding a quote that they understand and want to use for the activity. This can be done by using any search engine and typing "[key word] quote." For example, during a class session focused on describing one's past experiences you might do a *Quote Search* for "memories quote." The learners should then filter their results to see only images. This will provide them with a collection of topic-related quotes. The learners then peruse the quotes and choose one that they both understand and would like to use for the subsequent tasks.

There are a few directions this task can take. For example:
• Learners can be asked to rewrite the quote in their own words.
• Learners can agree or disagree with the quote, supporting their position with a reason.
• Learners can think of a story to explain the quote, either real or imagined.
• In pairs, learners could create a dialogue, where one of the characters speaks the words in that quote.

Variations

1. Learners could search for famous quotes in their first language and then try to translate or explain them in the target language.
2. Instead of a quote search, a search for "aphorisms" can be equally as effective.

Combinations

R-R-R　　*Hot Seat*　　*Co-op Remembering*

35. R-R-R

Read   **Refer**   **Remember**

Learning tasks

Reading   Writing   Expressing an opinion

Description

This is a structure for developing skills in writing and speaking. First, students produce something written (e.g., an answer to a question, an opinion on a topic, a summary of a group discussion, etc.).

Then, they find partners and share what they wrote. They do this with three different partners.

1. The first time, learners read what they wrote.
2. The second time, with a new partner, learners are allowed to refer to their writing but should endeavor to repeat most of it from memory.
3. The third time, with a different partner again, learners should remember what they wrote and not look at their writing.

Variations

1. A fourth partner can be added who takes the paper and quizzes the author on its contents.
2. Instead of using a self-created text, it's possible to use a written passage from a textbook or a handout. With this variation, however, the purpose is not to mechanically memorize each sentence. Rather, in stages two and three, learners should aim to synthesize the information and paraphrase the content in their own words.

Combinations

Di/Con/It   *Hot Seat*

36. Self-Sorting

Learning tasks

Warmer   Critical reflection

Description

Learners sort themselves into groups based on how they answer a question posed to the class.

First, the question is presented. Then, learners have some time to consider their own answer. Then they are instructed to stand up and find other people with a similar answer.

For example, if the lesson theme is leisure activities, you can ask, "How do you like to spend your free time?" Then, students sort themselves into groups. There may be a group for karaoke, a group for shopping, a group for outside activities, and a group for nothing in particular.

The instructor need not provide guidance as to what qualifies as "similar." Part of this structure's value lies in the learners identifying points of similarity and judging for themselves which answers are similar enough. Once groups have been formed, you can ask each to perform various tasks, such as explaining its organizing similarity or identifying the reasons for its shared answer. You can also keep the same groups and move into a new structure (e.g., *Writing Chain*, *1-by-1*, or *1-2-4 All*).

Variations

The task can be completed using gestures only, so that learners are only allowed to speak once they have already formed groups.

Combinations

Unique Questions   Hot Seat

37. Single-Sentence Stories

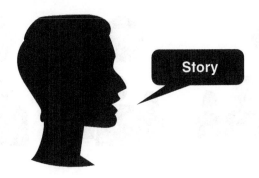

Learning tasks

Warmer   Grammar practice   Vocabulary learning

Description

The task is to tell a story using only one sentence. Depending on the level of the learners, the teacher can additionally ask that they use certain vocabulary words, or avoid using words like "and" in favor of more informative conjunctions (e.g., "so," "because"). The teacher can also suggest maximum or minimum time limits for each story. This is a great warm-up activity and need not be combined with another structure to be worthwhile—storytelling is a valuable skill to develop.

Variations

1. If you tell students to use a particular grammatical structure, this activity can help to review target language.
2. You can provide story prompts such as:
   1. I used to… / I never used to…
   2. …and I had never laughed so loud.
   3. …is the most embarrassing thing that has ever happened to me.

Combinations

Hot Seat   Writing Storm

38. Spectrum Questions

Learning tasks

Critical reflection   Expressing an opinion

Description

Each learner formulates a question or set of questions that can be answered on a scale from 1 to 10. For example: "How much do you enjoy speaking English?" where 1 = not at all and 10 = very much.

Before gathering responses to their questions, learners predict what the average response of the class will be. They write their prediction down and then survey some or all of the students in the class.

Once the responses have been collected, they compare the actual average with the predicted average. Learners can then identify the assumptions they had about the class and judge their accuracy.

Variations

1. The teacher can decide which number to aim for when creating the questions. For example, "Make a question in which the average answer will be 7." Or each group can be assigned a different number.
2. Learner A can present their questions to learner B. Then learner B must guess where learner A falls on the scale by asking probing questions.

Combinations

Need to Know   *Fact or Fiction*

39. Speedy Stories

Learning tasks

Discussion

Description

Learners prepare to tell a story. It can be a true story about a personal experience, a story about a family member or friend, or a story that they know from a movie or a book. They can note down some brief keywords to help them tell the story but should be discouraged from writing out the whole story in full. Tell the learners that they will need to spend four minutes telling their story.

Once they have prepared, put the learners in pairs. Keep strict track of time, and give one person four minutes to tell their whole story to their partner. Then switch roles and repeat.

After that, learners get a new partner. Repeat the task, but only give each learner three minutes to tell the story. They must tell it in full and not leave out any details.

Finally, change partners one more time and give each person only two minutes to tell the same story. The reduced time limit will mean that learners need to speak faster and increase their fluency.

Variations

1. The time limits can be adjusted (e.g., three minutes / two minutes / one minute)
2. After switching partners, learners can be told to repeat the story that they just heard from their previous partner rather than telling their own story again.

3. Instead of preparing a story to tell, learners can use a piece of writing that they have done in class. First, they try and remember the main points, and then they turn the paper over so that they cannot see it, and attempt to explain the content without looking.

Combinations

Hot Seat   *Cameraman Interview*   *Writing Storm*

40. Speedy Summaries

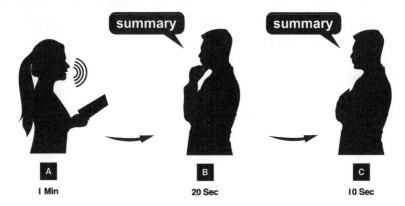

Learning tasks

Comprehension check   Expressing an opinion

Description

First, one learner tells a story or gives an opinion on a topic for one minute. The second learner listens and then summarizes what was said in twenty seconds. The third learner (or the first learner if working in a pair) then summarizes the summary in ten seconds.

    This pushes the learners to listen carefully, to identify the essential points, and to be concise with their language. It can be a follow-up to any structure that tasks the learners with thinking of a story or opinion, and it leads into any structures based on understanding the opinions of the other learners in the class.

Variations

This could be done as a group discussion. Groups discuss a question together for three minutes. Then, one group member summarizes their discussion in one minute. Then, the next member summarizes the summary in thirty seconds. They could also switch groups and give the summary to their new group.

Combinations

Single-Sentence Stories   *Choose and Use*   *Picture Role Play*

41. Storyboarding

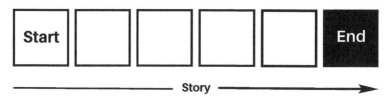

Learning tasks

Discussion   Brainstorming

Description

Storyboarding starts with learners drawing a set number of frames/boxes on a blank sheet of paper. Six is a good number for this, but anything from three to ten can be made to work. These boxes are a story frame, sequenced from beginning to end.

First, the content of the final box (the end of the story) is decided. This can be provided by the teacher, given by a partner, taken from the current unit in your coursebook, or left up to the individual (though it is best to provide some constraints to support creativity). The goal is to fill in the other frames leading up to the final one. Simple pictures are best, but keywords or phrases also work.

The story can be constructed from scratch or some sort of real situation can be used. An example of the latter would be giving the learners "You get your dream job" as the content for the final frame and then asking them to make their present situation the first frame.

Variations

1. You can begin by having learners fill in the content of any box, not just the last one.
2. It can be done individually, but it also works well in groups. This can be done as a *1-by-1* activity, in which each person in the group fills in the first frame only. Then, everyone's papers are rotated around the group, and students fill in the second frame of the paper they received, continuing the story. Papers then get rotated again, and so on until the stories are complete. In this case, it may be better to have students write sentences or captions to accompany the pictures.

3. *Online:* This can be orchestrated through a web-based slide presentation tool or a graphic design or note-taking platform. Many applications allow multiple users to work on a single document.

Combinations

R-R-R   Di/Con/It

42. Take Your Pick

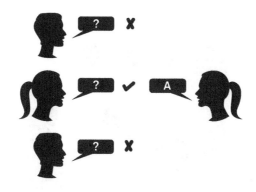

Learning tasks

Brainstorming   Discussion

Description

Put learners into groups of three or four in an interview situation. The interview starts with one student (the speaker) answering a question or sharing an opinion. Their group members then ask one follow-up question each. The speaker doesn't answer all the questions but instead picks one to answer. This cycle continues for a predetermined amount of time or rounds.

The questioners can be tasked with finding something out about the speaker, such as what they really think about a given topic. Combining *Take Your Pick* with a structure like *Fact or Fiction* creates a sort of adversarial interview in which each side benefits from thinking strategically.

Variations

Limit the kind of questions that can be asked to help reinforce certain grammar points or vocabulary (e.g., only ask questions in the past perfect).

Combinations

Fact or Fiction   *Ask, Answer, Add*

43. Teach It to Me

Learning tasks

Comprehension check   Predicting

Description

The learner is tasked with describing a concept on a piece of paper as though they were teaching it to a child. They can write, draw, use analogies, tell a story, etc.—whatever helps them to explain the concept. This is especially useful when the learners are trying to acquire some skill, such as finding the main idea or asking open-ended questions, as the need to distill their understanding will highlight the ways in which that understanding is lacking.

Variations

1. Learners can be required to use certain vocabulary words.
2. Learners can be required to use an analogy.
3. Learners can be required to use a story board.
4. One learner can feign complete ignorance about the topic and ask as many questions as they can.

Combinations

R-R-R   List and Switch   1-2-4 All

44. Topic Questions

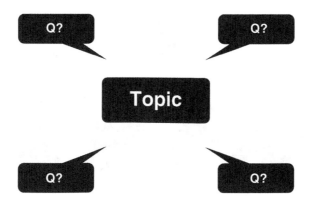

Learning tasks

Warmer   Predicting

Description

Learners are tasked with answering the question, "What should we learn about [topic]?" The topic in question here is one that will be covered in the class. This structure, then, works best when used before the topic has been explored.

The format of the learners' answers can be left up to them or you can ask them to phrase their answers in a particular way (e.g., as questions). For example, for a topic such as "giving advice," the learners might decide that they should learn how to ask if someone wants advice, how to give advice politely, and how to ask for advice.

Aside from serving as a warm-up or schema activation, this structure can have as much influence over how the class progresses as you are comfortable with. A group of curious students might populate the day's lesson with a checklist of valuable topics to cover, or you may only identify one that you can address. You might also use this structure as a lead-in for something broader. If you're willing to give the class significant free reign, the learners could choose one of their questions, work to answer it, and then share the answer.

Variations

As an alternative question, students can consider, "What do we already know about this topic?"

Combinations

Co-op Remembering   *Diamond 9*

45. Unique Questions

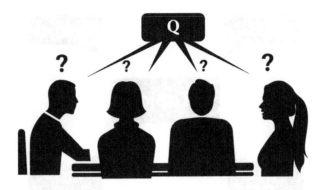

Learning tasks

Discussion   Vocabulary learning

Description

Learners are tasked with identifying a question they do not think anyone else will ask. This question can be about a shared topic or use a specified grammar point or vocabulary set. Learners then share questions and find out if theirs is unique.

When sharing, partners should answer the question. This structure can be iterated multiple times. For example, if the initial question is formed in groups, you might have one student from each group rotate to join a different group. Once questions have been shared, the rotated student remains in place and each group works to identify a new unique question so the structure can repeat.

Variations

1. You can break up all the groups and have students mingle, asking and answering their questions, and then return to their original group and share the unique questions they were asked.
2. This can be combined with *1-2-4 All* and questions can be determined by individuals, pairs, and groups.

Combinations

1-by-1   *Hot Seat*   *A & Q*

46. What's the Word?

Learning tasks

Vocabulary learning   Comprehension check

Description

Learners work in pairs or in groups. One student is the "guesser" while the other is the "hint giver." The guessers turn their backs so they can't see the board. The teacher then displays a word or phrase on the board. The hint givers see the word and then try to explain it so that their partner can guess the word. The teacher decides how hints can be given. For example, if the word is "automobile," hints can be given by:

- *Verbal description* (e.g., "This is a machine that transports people and things.")
- *Picture* (e.g., learner draws a picture of a car or a bus)
- *Gesture* (e.g., learner mimes driving a car)

This can be set up as an intra- or inter-team race. It can be done with time limits. Or it can be done with the hint giver choosing the word(s) to be guessed.

Variations

1. In a classroom where students share the same first language, rather than have one learner explain the word in English, they could give a translation in their first language.

2. In the case of verbal descriptions, the teacher can increase the challenge by adding words that cannot be used by the hint givers.

3. Pairs of hint givers can work as teams with both using the same kinds of hints, or by using complimentary hint styles (e.g., one draws, one gestures).

4. *Online:* In breakout rooms, having learners choose their own words/phrases to give hints about will work, or the teacher can write the word/phrase on a shared document that only the hint givers are allowed to look at. Once it has been guessed and the roles change, the hint givers can go to the next shared document.

Combinations

Choose and Use   *List and Switch*

47. Word Associations

Learning tasks

Vocabulary learning   Comprehension check

Description

This structure is most effective for reinforcing vocabulary. Its simplest incarnation has one learner choose a vocabulary word and then, without revealing what that word is, say words that are related to it. The other learner(s) tries to guess the vocabulary word. You can adjust the number of words the speaker is allowed to use depending on the level of the learners and the size of the vocabulary pool.

Variations

The flipped version of this structure has a learner present the vocabulary word, to which their partner responds with a related word or words. If done in groups, the responding students can take turns producing related words. Or you can task them with writing their related word so that everyone can reveal and compare what they wrote. This variation is a good lead-in to structures that task the learners with producing stories (e.g., *1-by-1: Build a Story, Single-Sentence Stories*) as they can be asked to use the vocabulary word(s) as well as the related words when constructing them.

Combinations

1-by-1: Build a Story   *Single-Sentence stories*

48. Writing Chain

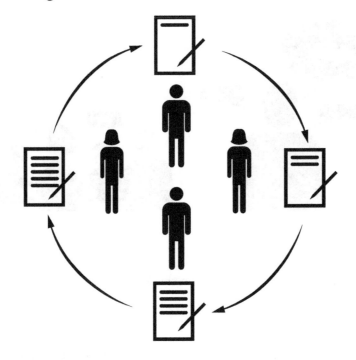

Learning tasks

Writing   Grammar practice

Description

Each learner starts with a piece of paper and some sort of prompt. They write one sentence responding to the prompt and then pass their paper to the next learner. The next person writes another sentence that builds on, responds to, or questions the first sentence. This continues for a set number of repetitions.

Variation can easily be introduced by changing whether the learners are all given the same prompt. If they are given the same prompt, it's an effective way to explore different perspectives. However, you can also start them with different prompts—perhaps the questions produced by a structure like *Unique Questions*.

Example prompts:
- Global warming
- Problems often faced by teenagers
- Once upon a time, there was a sad princess.
- How to get rich

Variations

1. This task can be used to create a fictional story, with learners instructed to include target vocabulary or grammatical structures.
2. Having learners use conjunctive adverbs at the beginning of each sentence provides practice in using these in writing. For example: *however, unfortunately, consequently, as a result, fortunately, etc.*

Combinations

Unique Questions   Di/Con/It

49. Writing Storm

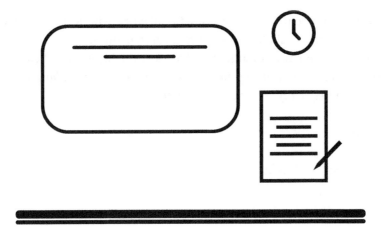

Learning tasks

Warmer   Brainstorming

Description

Learners are instructed to write non-stop for a specified amount of time. What they write can be related to a given topic or in response to a question, or it can be left up to them. The key point is that, for the duration of the writing period, their writing hand must not stop moving. Nonsense sentences are okay. Repetition is okay. Grammatical errors are okay. The use of erasers and dictionaries should be forbidden during the writing period (but may be used afterward if students rewrite or develop their brainstorm into a polished piece.)

This structure works well as a warm-up or as an introduction to a topic. It can also feed into structures that involve summarizing or answering questions about what was written, or as a follow-up to structures that produce a question or set of questions.

Variations

As a pair activity, this can also be a *Speaking Storm*. One learner can be tasked with speaking non-stop for a set period of time (one or two minutes is good to start with). The speaker must not stop speaking for the set time period. Their partner listens and notes down key points. Afterward, the note-taker summarizes the main points.

Combinations

Unique Questions   *R-R-R*

50. You Make the Rules

Learning tasks

Vocabulary learning   Comprehension check

Description

The learners count, as a group, from one to twenty-one, with each learner saying one number. The learner who says twenty-one gets to make a rule that replaces any of the numbers. The count then starts again. For example, "Instead of the number seven, tell us something that you did last weekend."

Anytime a rule is forgotten by the person counting, the count restarts with that person saying "one." The goal is to create as many rules as possible.

This structure is great for getting students engaged as: (1) they will not want to let their team down, and (2) they are making their own rules.

Some example rules:
- Tell us something that you did last weekend
- Give some advice on how to save money
- Make a sentence using the word "_____"
- Tell us a hope or a dream you have for the future
- Explain one of the main points from the reading passage

In order to keep the structure focused on the salient content, the teacher can establish restrictions on acceptable rules before the game starts (e.g., rules must be related to vocabulary from this list and/or rules must require past tense sentences).

Variations

1. Use a number other than twenty-one, or use a list of vocab words as the count.
2. Have groups write their rules on pieces of paper ahead of time and then switch. The person who says "twenty-one" chooses from the pre-written rules.

Combinations

Co-op Remembering   *Word Associations*   *Writing Storm*

Section 3

ADDITIONAL MATERIAL

Chapter 5

STRUCTURES FOR ASSESSMENT

These are structures that work particularly well for assessing students' understanding and getting feedback on their progress. Use these kinds of structures when you want to assess students' understanding of concrete concepts and content from the course.

Disagreements

Description

Learners work in groups to check their answers to questions. The assumption is that if everyone in the group agrees about the answer, then they are probably correct. It is only when disagreements are discovered that the instructor is brought in to provide correction.

This simple shift of burden to the learners can save time in that the instructor need not go over the answers to questions everyone already understands. It also keeps the learners engaged and thinking about their answers in comparison to those of their group, and helps develop an understanding of other learners as instructional resources, which improves the culture of the classroom.

Cold Call

Description

Cold Call is simply calling on a learner by name to answer a question posed by the instructor. There is nothing complicated about it, but, for some instructors, it can be difficult to begin using as it may seem confrontational.

There are two keys to making *Cold Call* work. First, use it enough that the learners come to expect it. Once it becomes a fixture of the class experience, it's much easier for everyone to deal with. Second, treat whatever response you get as valuable. Correct answers suggest that this particular learner understands the content. But a single correct answer should not regularly terminate the *Cold Call*. You might build on the answer by asking the same student or a different student to explain why the answer is correct. Before moving on, you should at least make sure that you can get a few correct answers in a row from different learners.

Incorrect answers are even more valuable. This is because they indicate an area of misunderstanding that you can address. But, perhaps more importantly, they provide an opportunity to cultivate a true learning culture in your classroom. Be positive about incorrect answers. Thank the student who gives one. Claim to love this particular mistake because it lets you explore the content in a particular way. Making this a regular feature of the class will have an enormous effect on the learners' willingness to make and admit mistakes.

When learners respond to a *Cold Call* by saying they don't know the answer, you have a similar cultural cultivation opportunity. Don't let the learner off the hook. Pry further to get their best guess or promise to come back to them with the same question after you call on a few other students with similar questions. In the latter case, make sure you do return to them.

Finger Answers

Description

This is an easy way to get an overall impression of how the learners are understanding the material with a limited set of possible answers. Simply assign numbers to the possible answers and have them report their answer by raising the corresponding number of fingers. For example, tell all learners who think the answer is "A" to raise one finger, and all learners who think the answer is "B" to raise two fingers.

In cases where you discover that there is a divide in how the learners answered, you can treat it as an opportunity to investigate. The best approach is to withhold the correct answer until you have explored the rationale for each of the possible answers. You want the learners to follow along with and participate in the thought process. If you give them the correct answer before doing this, they are less likely to pay attention and a learning opportunity may be missed.

Other physical responses for feedback are also possible. Ideas include:

- one hand on head / two hands on head / no hands on head
- raise right arm / raise left arm / raise both arms
- stand up / remain seated

And if you're in a silly mood, or the class needs some livening up:

- moo like a cow / bark like a dog / cluck like a chicken

Respond and Sit

Description

This is a particularly effective structure to use with learners who are shy or unwilling to volunteer answers in class. When brainstorming ideas or eliciting as many answers as possible on an open-ended question, first have all the learners stand up. Tell them that whoever calls out an idea is allowed to sit down.

While learners may have been embarrassed to volunteer an answer initially, it's even more embarrassing to be the last one left standing after everyone else has answered. So, learners will suddenly become very keen to tell you their ideas.

In larger classes, you can put students in groups. When any one member of the group calls out an idea, the whole group may sit down.

Question Storming

Description

Learners brainstorm questions they can ask about some topic or material. On a sheet of paper, in pairs or in groups, learners write as many questions as they can *to which they do not know the answers.* Questions can be related to the meaning of words or expressions, the accurate use of grammar, the content of something in the textbook, or just a general question related to the theme of the lesson.

This can be very useful when the learners do not seem to sufficiently understand the material but no one is willing to ask any questions. After the brainstorming period, the teacher can elicit questions to address or the learners can be asked to switch questions and attempt to answer the ones they end up with.

(This structure can also be used outside of the *Structures for Assessment* context.)

Chapter 6

EVOLUTIONS

This chapter provides several ideas for evolving structures to focus on different patterns of interaction or else to make them a little more complex. Evolutions can be applied to all of the structures in this book to enhance interaction, deepen understanding, and increase the challenge if learners appear ready for added complexity. Here are just a few suggestions for how some structures can be evolved.

RTQ

RTQ stands for "repeat the question." In this evolution, the learner is asked to answer a question by using the wording of the question in their answer. For example, if the question is "What is your favorite food?" the answer could be "My favorite food is pizza."

Plus Alpha

This evolution tasks the learner with providing additional information beyond what is explicitly required to answer the question they were asked. Restrictions such as "use a vocabulary word" can be added.

FUQs

This evolution tasks the learner with asking a follow-up question (FUQ) about what their partner said. Restrictions such as "Don't ask 'why'" can be added.

Summarize

This evolution tasks the learner with summarizing what the previous learner said before taking his or her own turn.

Empathize

The learner responds to a previous learner by attempting to identify the underlying or emotional subtext of what was said. Examples include: "It sounds like you had a busy weekend," and "You sound relieved to be finished."

Feedback

The learner responds to what was said by providing feedback. Have the learners use a phrase such as, "What if you tried…" to introduce the feedback.

Yes, and…

The learner responds to the previous learner with the phrase "Yes, and…" before adding something that is relevant to what was said. It is important that these relevant additions not be limited to those that support the previous point. Responding to "Summer is the most fun season" with "Yes, and winter has the best holidays" would be both logically consistent and a way to stretch the divergent thinking of the learners.

Yes/No—Why

Yes/No—Why asks the learners to address a point by agreeing or disagreeing with it and then supporting their position with reasons, examples, etc.

Chapter 7

EXAMPLES OF LESSON SEQUENCES

In this chapter are some examples of how a FERM-structured lesson may unfold. There are countless ways in which FERM structures can be combined into lesson sequences. The structures that are chosen, and the way in which they are combined, will depend upon the aims of the course, the focus of the lesson, and the needs of the learners. When first starting out with the FERM approach, you may want to prepare a rough flow of structures before the class begins. However, we believe that very often it's better to leave the lesson unplanned. As you become more familiar with these structures, you'll be able to create the flow as you teach the lesson.

Below are a few examples of sequences. These are not lesson plans, but examples of how your lesson may take shape in real time, as you observe and interact with learners.

Lesson Example: Free Time Activities

> **Target vocabulary**: What do [or don't] you like to do?; I often, I sometimes, I never; read books, watch movies, listen to music
> **Target grammar**: Expressing likes and dislikes in full sentences; adverbs of frequency

FERM Flow Number One

1-by-1 describe and guess

Learner 1 (L1) chooses and describes one of the phrases from a vocabulary list of free time activities. Learner 2 (L2) guesses the phrase.
(About two minutes, in pairs or triads.)

1-by-1 Uno

L1 makes a sentence using a vocabulary word and the target grammar (e.g., "I don't like to read books"). L2 keeps either the grammar or the vocab word and changes the other (e.g., "I don't like to listen to music").
(About two minutes, small groups.)

A & Q

The learners stand up and move around freely making pairs. L1 names a free time activity (e.g., "watch movies"). L2 tries to guess how L1 feels about the activity by asking a question (e.g., "What do you like to do?"). L1 confirms or disconfirms the guess.

+ FUQs

L2 asks a FUQ (e.g., "What kind of movies are your favorite?"). L1 answers. They switch roles. When finished, they find a new partner.
(About five minutes, pairs or triads.)

50/50 Questions

The learners formulate one to three *50/50 Questions* based upon what they learned during the *A & Q* task.

+ Plus Alpha

They ask and answer these questions, adding additional information.

+ FUQs

They ask each other FUQs.
They record the answers they are given. When the time is up, they work with their partner(s) to see how close they got to a 50/50 split.
(About two minutes to decide questions in pairs or triads, five minutes to ask and answer as a whole class.)

Devil vs. Angel

The questions that got closest to 50/50 are identified. Roles are decided. Two students take opposite positions and try to convince the listener(s) for two minutes. The listener(s) then give their opinion for one minute. Switch roles and questions and repeat at least once.
(About three minutes total, in groups of three or four, repeated at least once.)

FERM Flow Number Two

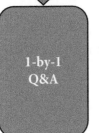

The learners find out they will be studying language related to free time activities. They spend two minutes trying to guess what grammar and vocabulary this might consist of.

Predict the material

+ Cold Call

The teacher calls on learners to get some ideas before going to the text to see how accurate their predictions were.
(About two minutes predicting, one minute check for understanding, in pairs.)

L1 asks a question using one of the grammar points
(e.g., "What do you love to do in your free time?")

1-by-1 Q&A

+ RTQ

L2 repeats the question (*RTQ*) and answers (e.g., "In my free time, I love to play with my dog.") L1 or L3 then answers the same question. L2 then asks the next question.
(About two minutes, in pairs or triads.)

Imaginary friend

The learners use the website thispersondoesnotexist.com (or the teacher provides pictures for them to use). They write five sentences about their imaginary friend's free time preferences using at least three vocabulary words.
(Individually, about three minutes.)

RRR

The learners make pairs or triads. L1 reads what they wrote and then answers a FUQ from each partner. Each person has a turn. Then new pairs are formed. The learners try to remember what they wrote but are allowed to refer to it if they forget. Then, in the third round, they cannot use their paper at all.
(About five minutes, in pairs or triads.)

Expert interview

Each learner takes a turn answering questions from their group about the free time preferences of their imaginary friend.
(About two minutes per round, small groups.)

Lesson Example: Past Experiences

>**Target vocabulary**: for, ago, since
>**Target grammar**: past tense, present perfect tense

FERM Flow Number One

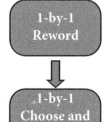

L1 makes a sentence using past or present perfect tense.
L2 rewords the sentence using the other tense.
(About two minutes, in pairs.)

L1 chooses "for," "since," or "ago" and an activity. L2 makes a sentence using these.
(About two minutes, in pairs.)

Each group identifies a unique question that uses "for," "since," or "ago" and one of the two tenses.

+ Plus Alpha

One person from each group rotates and asks each member of their new group the question. These learners answer with additional information. The cycle repeats two more times.
(Two minutes to think of questions, two minutes to ask and answer them, three rounds, small groups.)

The learners work together to remember and list all the questions they asked or answered.
(About two minutes, small groups.)

L1 is asked questions on the topic of their past experiences by their group members. Each group member asks a question, and L1 chooses which one to answer. This style of interview continues for two minutes before roles are switched. The list of remembered unique questions should be used as inspiration.
(About two minutes each round, small groups.)

FERM Flow Number Two

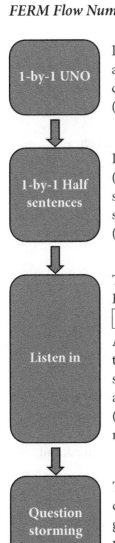

1-by-1 UNO

L1 makes a sentence that combines "for," "since," or "ago" with an experience or activity. L2 keeps one of these elements and changes the other to make a new sentence.
(About two minutes, small groups.)

1-by-1 Half sentences

L1 starts a sentence but breaks it off around halfway through (e.g., "Five years ago…"). L2 finishes the sentence (e.g., "…I started studying English"). L2 starts the next sentence. Each sentence has to use "for," "ago," or "since."
(About two minutes, small groups.)

Listen in

Two learners discuss, for example, their history studying English while one or two others listen.

+ Summarize

After two minutes, the listeners summarize the conversation to the speakers, including anything they didn't understand or still want to know. Switch roles and repeat so each person gets a chance at conversation.
(About two minutes conversation, one minute summary, two rounds, small groups.)

Question storming

The learners brainstorm questions they can ask their classmates about their history studying English. If possible, getting everyone to write their ideas on a shared resource will push their creativity and give them more options.
(About three minutes, in pairs or small groups.)

Ask, Answer, Add

The learners start with a simple statement like "I've been studying English since elementary school." They answer a FUQ from a partner and add the information from their answer to their next initial statement. They go through as many rounds as they can, lengthening their initial statement each time.
(About five minutes, whole class mingling.)

The learners consider their history studying English and describe their relationship to it metaphorically by finishing the sentence, "For me, studying English is like…"
(About two minutes, individual.)

Lesson Example: Giving Directions

Target vocabulary: straight, on the left/right, across from, next to
Target grammar: Imperatives

FERM Flow Number One

The learners are told the next unit is on giving directions and are asked to predict what kind of language they will learn.

+ 1-2-4 All

Learners work on their own, then in pairs, then again in small groups.
(About one minute on their own, one minute in pairs, then two minutes in small groups.)

+ List and Switch

Groups compile a written list of their predicted language. These lists are switched between groups, who try to add something else to them. This may be a good time to use the textbooks to compare and add so that none of the required language is missed.
(About five minutes, groups.)

The lists go back to the original groups who created them. They do *1-by-1: Build a Story,* wherein they start with a question like, "Where is the post office?" and each member uses one of the language items from the list to make a sentence to answer the question. Each sentence should be a continuation of the one that came before it.

+ Summarize

After a certain number of turns, the learner who asked the initial question should try to summarize the directions they received. The next learner asks a new question and the cycle repeats.
(About five minutes, groups.)

Co-operative listening

The learners pair up. One is tasked with taking notes, the other with remembering. The teacher gives directions on how to get somewhere while the note taker writes notes and their partner tries to listen and remember what is said. The pair shares what they have.
(About five minutes, pairs.)

+ Disagreements

Each pair then compares with another pair, filling in what they missed and identifying any disagreements they have. The teacher asks for any disagreements and settles them by sharing what was actually said.
(About five minutes, groups.)

1-by-1 Expanding sentences

In small groups, learners attempt to answer requests for directions from one of the members. The first learner makes one sentence giving directions. The next repeats what was already said before adding a sentence. This goes on until the series of directions becomes impossible to remember, which triggers a restart.
(About five minutes, groups.)

50–50 Quiz

Learners choose a location on or close to campus. They write directions from the classroom to that location. The location and directions should be such that half of the class will be able to guess the location on their first try.
(About five minutes, pairs.)

+R-R-R

Each learner presents their directions to three others, reading them the first time, referencing them the second, and remembering them the third. The student who is listening tries to guess the location, and can ask FUQs if stumped.
(About ten minutes, rotating pairs.)

FERM Flow Number Two

Each learner is given a piece of paper and told that the lesson will be covering how to give directions. They think about what they will probably learn.

They are asked to write one word or phrase that they expect to learn before passing their paper to the next person. No repeats are allowed.
(About two minutes, small groups.)

The papers are flipped over and the learners take turns remembering something that the group wrote down.
(About two minutes, small groups.)

In pairs, one learner holds one of the papers from the previous steps and quizzes the other partner, who must physically represent the chosen word or phrase (e.g., "go straight" could be represented by pointing ahead of oneself). The roles switch after two minutes.
(About four minutes, pairs.)

In groups of three or four, the first learner spends a minute explaining how to get to a place of their choosing. The next learner summarizes these directions in twenty seconds. And the third leaner tries to do it in ten seconds. Roles are switched until everyone gets a chance to go.
(About six minutes, small groups.)

In the same groups, one learner begins as the "local expert" and the other three are "tourists" who are asking directions to various places with the option to ask follow-up questions as well. Roles are switched every two minutes.
(About six minutes, small groups.)

Lesson Example: Making Guesses

Target vocabulary: could be, must be, might be, can't be
Target grammar: Modals of deduction

FERM Flow Number One

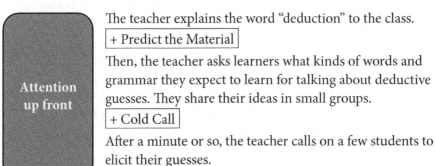

Attention up front

The teacher explains the word "deduction" to the class.
+ Predict the Material

Then, the teacher asks learners what kinds of words and grammar they expect to learn for talking about deductive guesses. They share their ideas in small groups.
+ Cold Call

After a minute or so, the teacher calls on a few students to elicit their guesses.
(About four minutes, whole class and small groups.)

Attention up front

The teacher explains the modals of deduction, perhaps getting the students to identify what degree of certainty they express.
(About five minutes, whole class.)

1-by-1 Different

The students make sentences using the modals of deduction. They are not allowed to repeat any of them until they have all been used. Continue for two minutes.
(About four minutes, pairs or small groups.)

1-by-1 UNO

In the same groups, a student makes a sentence with a modal of deduction and a prediction. The next student has to keep either the modal or the prediction while changing the other one. Continue for two minutes.
(About four minutes, small groups.)

Picture role play

In pairs, students choose a random picture to role play. This can be taken from the coursebook or found online.

+ Listen In

In groups of three or four, the pair role plays their picture for two minutes while the other group members observe. When the time ends, the observers use the modals of deduction to make guesses about the identity of the speakers and context of the role play. The role players confirm or deny these guesses and can give hints as they see fit until, after two minutes, the picture is revealed and the next pair starts their role play. (About eight minutes, small groups.)

FERM Flow Number Two

Predict the material

The teacher shares that the class will be about making guesses and asks students to think about what they might learn.

+ Respond and Sit

All the students stand up and, when they make a prediction about what language will be covered, they can sit down. (About four minutes, whole class.)

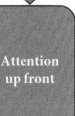

Attention up front

The teacher explains the modals of deduction.

+ Question Storming

While listening, students think of as many questions as they can about the teacher's explanation.

+ Cold Call

The teacher calls on some students to ask a question. (About five minutes, whole class.)

A & Q

The students make one statement for each of the modals. They share these statements with a partner, who makes a suitable question to match it. (e.g., L1: "She might be sick." L2: "Why is Lisa absent today?") (About five minutes, pairs.)

1-by-1 Choose and use

One student chooses one of the modals and the next two students each make a sentence using that modal. (About three minutes, small groups.)

Collecting answers

Each student chooses one of the statements they wrote for A & Q (or writes a new one). They stand up and share it with a partner who responds with a guess using one of the modals (e.g., L1: "My teacher is an alien. What do you think about that?" L2: "She must be in disguise.")

After they have both had a turn, the student finds a new partner, shares their statement and any previous responses that have been made, and asks, "What do you think about that?" (e.g., L1: "My teacher is an alien. She must be in disguise. What do you think about that?" L3: "She could be from Mars."). (About five minutes, rotating pairs.)

BIBLIOGRAPHY

Altuwairesh, Nasrin. "Deliberate Practice in Second Language Learning: A Concept Whose Time Has Come." *International Journal of Language and Linguistics* 4, no. 3 (2017): 111–115.

Coyle, Daniel. *The Culture Code*. New York: Bantam Books, 2019.

Cronkleton, Emily. "Time under Tension Workouts: Are They More Effective?" Accessed March 28, 2023. https://www.healthline.com/health/exercise-fitness/time-under-tension

Dörnyei, Zoltán. *Motivational Strategies in the Language Classroom*. Cambridge: Cambridge University Press, 2011.

Dörnyei, Zoltán and Tim Murphey. *Group Dynamics in the Language Classroom*. Cambridge: Cambridge University Press, 2003.

Edmonson, Amy. "Psychological Safety and Learning Behavior in Work Teams." *Administrative Science Quarterly* 44, no. 2 (1999): 350–83. https://doi.org/10.2307/2666999

Edmonson, Amy. *The Fearless Organization: Creating Psychological Safety in the Workplace for Learning, Innovation, and Growth*. Hoboken: John Wiley & Sons, Inc., 2018.

Ellis, Rod. *Reflections on Task-Based Language Teaching*. Bristol: Multilingual Matters, 2018.

Ericsson, Anders, Ralf Krampe, and Clemens Tesch-Römer. "The Role of Deliberate Practice in the Acquisition of Expert Performance," *Psychological Review* 100, no. 3 (1993): 363–406.

Harlen, Wynne. "On the Relationship between Assessment for Formative and Summative Purposes." In John Gardner (ed.), *Assessment and Learning* (2nd ed.). London: Sage, 2012: 87–102.

Hattie, John and Helen Timperley. "The Power of Feedback," *Review of Educational Research* 77, no. 1 (2007): 81–112.

Johnson, Steven. *Where Good Ideas Come From: The Natural History of Innovation*. New York: Riverhead Books, 2010.

Kauffman, Stuart. *At Home in the Universe: The Search for Laws of Self-Organization and Complexity*. Oxford: Oxford University Press, 1995.

Lemov, Doug, Erica Woolway, Katie Yezzi, and Dan Heath. *Practice Perfect: 42 Rules for Getting Better at Getting Better*. San Francisco: Jossey-Bass, 2012.

Larsen-Freeman, Diane, and Lynne Cameron. *Complex Systems and Applied Linguistics*. Oxford: Oxford University Press, 2008.

Lawley, James, and Penny Tompkins. *Metaphors in Mind: Transformation through Symbolic Modelling*. London: The Developing Company Press, 2000.

Li, Shaofeng. "The Effectiveness of Corrective Feedback in SLA: A Meta-Analysis," *Language Learning* 60, no. 2 (2010): 309–365.

Lightbown, Patsy and Nina Spada. *How Languages Are Learned*. Oxford: Oxford University Press, 2013.

Lipmanowicz, Henri, and Keith McCandless. *The Surprising Power of Liberating Structures*. Liberating Structures Press, 2014.

Lipmanowicz, Henri and Keith McCandless. "Liberating Structures." Accessed March 6, 2023. liberatingstructures.com

Loewen, Shawn. *Introduction to Instructed Second Language Acquisition* (2nd ed.). New York: Routledge, 2020.

Long, Michael. "The Role of the Linguistic Environment in Second Language Acquisition." In *Handbook of Second Language Acquisition*, ed. William Ritchie and Tej Bhatia. San Francisco: Academic Press, 1996, 413–468.

Meddings, Luke, and Scott Thornbury. *Teaching Unplugged*. Surrey, UK: Delta Publishing, 2015.

Nation, Paul. *Learning Vocabulary in Another Language* (2nd ed.). Cambridge: Cambridge University Press, 2013.

Palmer, Parker. *To Know as We Are Known: Education as a Spiritual Journey*. San Francisco: Harper, 1983.

Rose, Don. "Unit Training Management." *NCO Journal* (March, 2020): 1–5. Accessed March 30, 2023. https://www.armyupress.army.mil/Portals/7/nco-journal/images/2020/March/Unit-Training/unit-training-management.pdf.

Ruiz-Primo, Marai Araceli and Susan Brookhart. *Using Feedback to Improve Learning*. New York: Routledge, 2018.

Singhal, Arvind, Lauren Perez, Kristin Stevik, Erik Monness, and Peer Jacob Svenkerud, "Liberating Structures as Pedagogical Innovation for Inclusive Learning: A Pilot Study in a Norwegian University." *Journal of Creative Communications* 15, no. 1 (2020): 1.

Stanier, Michael Bungay. *The Coaching Habit*. Toronto: Box of Crayons Press, 2016.

Vygotsky, Lev. *Mind in Society: The Development of Higher Psychological Processes*. Cambridge: Harvard University Press, 1978.

Printed and bound by CPI Group (UK) Ltd, Croydon, CR0 4YY

09/06/2025

14686147-0002

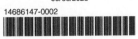